A history of a West Wales village

Llanfallteg

First Published 2009.

ISBN 978-0-9562134-0-2

Copyright of the Llanfallteg History Society

Printed in Wales

By Dimond Press, Pembroke

Foreword

I have before me a copy of the notice of the Annual General Meeting of the Pembrokeshire and Carmarthenshire Otterhounds, 11.00 a.m. Wednesday 3rd August 1977, at the Railway Inn, Llanfallteg. I was actually there, more than 30 years ago which makes me feel an anachronistic part of history.

This History of Llanfallteg has been compiled by members of the community, about the community and for the community. This probably explains why Llanfallteg thrives whilst similar villages become dry dormitories for commuters. The dedicated, caring research and enthusiasm of the contributors breathes vibrancy into these pages.

History can easily be reduced to a recital of dry facts. Not here, the pulse of the living village can be felt across the ages. This history assures us of the future of the village.

I congratulate the authors and commend the book to any with a passing acquaintance with Llanfallteg.

Richard Griffiths.

Acknowledgements

We would like to thank Awards for All Wales for the grant funding that made this book possible, and Pauline Griffiths from the Wilson Museum, Narberth who supported the grant application.

Among those who have given help and advice are Jenny Hall and Paul Sambrook of Trysor who helped us to structure the book and helped with some historical content.

Many locals, too numerous to mention by name, have provided information. Willy Reynolds of Penybont deserves our special thanks for the enormous amount of information that he has provided. Willy '*Bont*' has lived in the village for most of the 20th century and his recollections have been invaluable.

We are grateful to Vernon Beynon for his contribution on local knowledge, to Peter Icke for drawing many of the maps and to John Spencer for his photographs and his research.

Many thanks also to the staff at Pembrokehire Record Office, Carmarthenshire Record Office, Haverfordwest Library, Carmarthen Library, the National Library of Wales, Cambria Archeology and Royal Commission on the Ancient and Historical Monuments of Wales (RCAHMW.).

We have attempted to present the story of Llanfallteg as coherently as possible, but the book is the collective work of several writers, with their own individual styles. Any errors are ours, although in our defence, information in old documents is sometimes conflicting and archaeological interpretations change over time.

Finally we would like to thank our families for contending with our time spent on research, meetings, writings and the lots of paperwork which it all entailed.

Contents

PREFACE

Llanfallteg may seem like an ordinary village, but it has seen some interesting times: once a Roman road came nearby. The Black Death struck, there were various religious and social upheavals, and even a battle in the 13th century.

Change in the last century has been remarkable. Somebody living in the village a hundred years ago would have been more familiar with the life of people 2000 years ago than with that of modern times. The exponential rate of technological change has altered village life beyond recognition. Piped water only arrived in 1935 and electricity in the late 1950s, whilst central heating wasn't within the reach of people on average incomes until the 1970s.

Good health has increased greatly. A hundred years ago 10% of babies died before their first birthday; now the death rate is 1 in 200. A time traveller going back to the 1920s for a holiday in Llanfallteg would be advised to have numerous vaccinations including typhoid, diphtheria, hepatitis and tuberculosis, as well as being advised to boil the water before drinking it.

The two World Wars changed the expectations of the young men who travelled away from home, probably for the first time. Mechanisation reduced the need for labour on farms and people left in their droves for better-paid jobs and more comfortable lives until as recently as the 1970s. Llanfallteg, in common with many other villages in Wales, became a ghost town, with homes falling into disrepair, churches and chapels closing and farming methods changing.

Transport has changed dramatically. Llanfallteg was a *'railway town'*. The arrival of the railways in the 19th century changed the shape of the village, both physically, with extra building close to the station, and economically. The railway brought cheap goods into the area, destroying local livelihoods that were dependent on cottage industries. The railway brought prosperity for some, but also hastened the decline of many rural trades and the fortunes of the people who practised them.

Motor transport killed off the railways, but also helped revive the village, allowing people to commute to work whilst living in a rural environment. The village is vibrant again, but the culture has changed. Most newcomers are not Welsh speakers, and although the children learn Welsh at school, it is their second language.

Now we have the telephone, internet, hospitals with modern drugs to treat nearly all ailments and supermarkets providing food of every kind, whether it is in or out of season. Unfortunately the resources necessary to maintain this modern lifestyle are unsustainable and as history has a habit of repeating itself, you wonder if someday people in the village will be living in a similar way to our predecessors, relying heavily on agriculture and growing most of their own food.

The names of some places have changed over the years, and on occasion, somebody has moved and taken their house name with them! We have used the modern name throughout the book, but we have also tried to give previous place names at some point in the book. The spelling of names has been a particular issue: should it be *Waun Delyn*, *Waun-delyn,* or concatenated to *Waundelyn*. Generally we have used the latter unless the generally accepted spelling is different. Old spellings of place names are in italics.

Members of the Llanfallteg History and Heritage Group have researched the village history over many months. Some areas are well documented, such as Tegfynydd Mansion, but details of the lives of many people were unrecorded until the tithe schedules were drawn up in 1843 from maps made between 1790 and 1830, and the 1841 census.

Sources are listed at the end of each chapter, but for the sake of brevity the vast amounts of documentation available in the Carmarthenshire and Pembrokeshire Records Offices have not been mentioned individually. They are available to read in the Records Offices, catalogued by property name. Similarly, electoral roll, census and tithe schedule records are not listed.

There is still a lot to discover about the village and the neighbourhood. If this book has whetted your appetite, the Llanfallteg History Group arranges monthly trips to sites of historical interest. All are welcome.

INTRODUCTION

The parish of Llanfallteg

Like many communities on county boundaries Llanfallteg has had its fair share of boundary changes. Currently the whole of the community lies in the county of Carmarthenshire, but in the not too distant past, a significant part lay in Pembrokeshire and as a result Llanfallteg (Carmarthenshire) and Llanfallteg West (Pembrokeshire) are often both marked on maps, although they are one community, with the river Tâf neatly dissecting the two parts.

Llanfallteg has been spelt in a number of ways. One of the earliest spelling being Llanveltheg in 1398 and the spelling was Llanfalteg in the railway timetable. Several hamlets make up Llanfallteg - old Llanfallteg around the church, Rhyd-ddol-esgob around The Plash, Rhydywrach and Hiraeth.

Llanfallteg is part of the modern community of Henllanfallteg, lying at the western extremity of the County of Carmarthenshire, some 15 miles west of the county town. It comprises the old parishes of Henllan Amgoed, Llanfallteg, Llanfallteg West and parts of the original parishes of Llangan, Cilymaenllwyd and Llanboidy.

This book is about the history of Llanfallteg. The first part describes the area from ancient times to the modern day, the second part is an historical '*walk*' from Glanrhyd in the south up through the village centre and ending at Hiraeth.

Physical Environment

The land is generally low-lying with elevations above sea level ranging from 160 metres in the north-east of the parish to below 30 metres along the valley of the River Tâf to the south. The underlying rocks are sediments laid down under the sea in the Ordovician period between 450 and 490 million years ago. At that time the area was in the southern hemisphere at the same latitude as modern - day South

Africa, in an ocean just off the coast of Laurentia (now North America). Trilobites were the predominant animals at the start of the Ordovician period but they were starting to decline, being replaced by molluscs such as Brachiopods.

The present landscape shows evidence of glaciation, the low hills to the north being rounded from the action of the ice, whilst the valleys are U-shaped in section and there is surface evidence of glacial deposition. The topsoils were laid down during the last glaciation, which peaked about 20,000 years ago, range from heavy, wet clays to lighter, well-drained sands in the south. There are also recently formed areas of peat and river alluvium. The lighter soils, about 30-40% of the total, were used for arable crops in the more favoured areas but the majority of the land is given over to grass production.

Llanfallteg has a climate that is usually described as maritime: summers tend to be cool and damp and winters mild and wet. Snowfall is minimal and severe frosts rare, as are hot, dry spells. During winter, severe westerly gales are common. This results in a countryside that is lush and green and quite well wooded.

Location

Llanfallteg is best approached from the south by leaving the A40 at Llanddewi Velfrey and following the minor road northwards. Fine views across the parish with the Preseli Hills as a backdrop can be seen from here on clear days. The nearest settlements of any size are Llandissilio to the north-west, Clynderwen to the west, Narberth to the south-west, Whitland to the south-east and Llanboidy to the north.

The A40 trunk road runs just to the south of the area and the A478 Cardigan road is less than a mile to the west. There are no major roads within the parish itself however, which means that there is very little through traffic. The Haverfordwest - Carmarthen railway line just skirts the southern boundary. These facts, combined with an absence of heavy industry in the vicinity, result in a generally tranquil environment for the inhabitants.

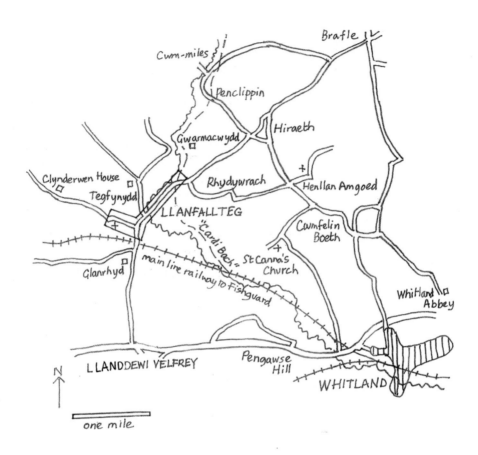

Llanfallteg and District

Sources

British Geological Survey

www.visionofbritain.org.uk

EARLY TIMES

Periods	Timescale	Description	Local evidence
Stone Age: Palaeolithic	2.6 million years ago to about 10,000 years ago	99% of human evolution, other human species, Neanderthals. Hunter gatherers	Human habitation at Coygan cave, 38,000 years ago
Stone age: Mesolithic	10,000 to 6,000 years ago	Period since end of last ice age. Hunter gatherers. Start of Stonehenge	No evidence in Llanfallteg, Bluestones for Stonehenge moved from Carn Menyn in the Preselis
Stone age: Neolithic	From about 4500 B.C. in north west Europe	Forest clearance, settlements develop, agriculture: livestock and crops	Cromlechs at Cefn Brafle and Gwal y Filiast. Stone axe from Parke
Bronze Age	2100 – 700 B.C.	Bronze tools and weapons, although stone also used	Round barrows at Ddol Garn and Parc y Crug.
Iron Age	800 B.C to Roman Conquest	Iron tools and weapons developed	Local hillforts, enclosures at Llangan

The Stone Ages

To take a walk through what is now the area of Llanfallteg during the last Ice Age, some 25,000 years ago, would have been a very interesting experience. Large animals such as mammoth, woolly rhinoceros, reindeer and bison roamed the barren landscape and were preyed upon by bear, hyena and wolf. Remains of these creatures have been discovered in Coygan Cave, between Pendine and Laugharne, just eight or nine miles to the southeast. In the same cave, evidence of human occupation, dating to 38,000 years ago, has also been found in the form of flint implements. Populations of these Palaeolithic peoples would have been very small; just a few dozen throughout the whole of Wales, mainly inhabiting caves, so it is highly unlikely that there would have been any permanent human habitation in what is now West Wales at this time.

From 11,500 years ago, the climate began to warm and sea levels began to rise. Over the following two thousand years, the land became covered with thick forests of broadleaved trees. The people of this Mesolithic period exploited these forests as hunting grounds and began to build shelters. Their way of life was that of nomadic hunter-gatherers. They made beautifully crafted weapons from flint, stone and bone to fish and hunt, and the forests would have provided an ample supply of plant foods in season - nuts, fruits, roots and fungi. The transient lifestyles of these Palaeolithic and Mesolithic peoples resulted in their leaving very few traces of their existence and certainly none have been found within the parish of Llanfallteg itself.

About 6,000 years ago a new wave of ideas and technology arrived from the European mainland. The Neolithic or New Stone Age period saw a dramatic change in the landscape over a period of a thousand years or so as the forests began to be cleared. The livelihoods of Neolithic peoples were predominantly based on farming rather than hunter-gathering, so they lived in settled communities, tied to the land by their crops and domesticated animals.

Although there is no evidence of permanent Neolithic settlement within Llanfallteg, just to the north, near Llanglydwen, there is a fairly well preserved cromlech or burial chamber known as Gwal y Filiast. A less well-preserved cromlech is to be found at Cefn Brafle, Crosshands and Llanboidy. Cromlechs were the communal graves of settled Neolithic peoples and their existence is always a strong indication that there were people living in the vicinity at this time.

Gwal y Filiast (John Spencer)

Unfortunately, there is little archaeological evidence of the nature and location of Neolithic settlements in the region. The only Neolithic artefact found locally is a stone axe discovered at Parke in 1953. Neolithic people still used flint and stone tools and their stone axes were perfected to enable them to clear the forests for agriculture. The axe found near Parke was made of stone found in North Wales, a reminder of the important trade in stone axes that spanned the British Isles during this period.

The Bronze Age

About 4000 years ago, another great technological leap took place with the introduction of metalworking into Britain. This appears to have been the result of the movement of peoples from the Continent, bringing with them new ideas. The ability to extract and work in metals, initially copper, then later the more durable bronze, led to significant changes in the way humans could interact with their environment.

However, stone and flint tools continued to be used throughout the Bronze Age.

In the Llanfallteg area, an implement of this period was found in a quarry near Lan Farm and is now in Tenby Museum. It is described as a large axe-hammer as it has a vertical cutting edge that would have been in line with the haft and a rounded butt-end for hammering. Manufactured from Preseli greenstone, it is 7.5 inches long, very symmetrically shaped and worked to a smooth but unpolished surface. On examination, it can be seen that the maker intended it to have a wooden shaft and began to drill holes about 1.5 inches in diameter in its top. The job was not completed however, probably due to the fact that the two holes are out of alignment and would have resulted in a badly fitting haft. We therefore have a 4000 year old reject which nevertheless remains in good condition, as it was never used!

Stone axe found at Lan (Tenby Museum)

Another similar axe-hammer, this time fully perforated, has been found nearby at Marchgwyn, Cilymaenlwyd.

Local place names suggest that there may have been a number of Bronze Age round barrows or burial mounds within the community. These include Ddol Garn and Park y Crug, whilst names such as Maen Llwyd and Park Main may show where Bronze Age standing stones once existed. Such sites are important to our understanding of Bronze Age society as archaeologists have found that they are funerary monuments, associated with the burial of the cremated remains of the dead.

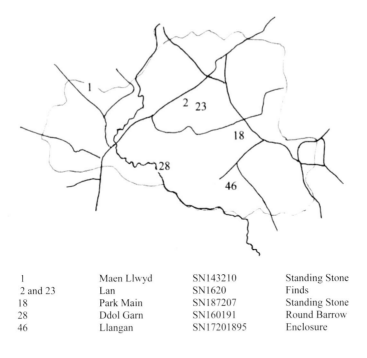

1	Maen Llwyd	SN143210	Standing Stone
2 and 23	Lan	SN1620	Finds
18	Park Main	SN187207	Standing Stone
28	Ddol Garn	SN160191	Round Barrow
46	Llangan	SN17201895	Enclosure

Map of Bronze Age sites

Surviving examples of both round barrows and standing stones are known in neighbouring communities, such as the large round barrow at Bryn Dwyrain, just south of Llanfallteg West. At the nearby hamlet of Crosshands, Llanboidy, two round barrows were excavated in 1925. They both contained evidence of cremation burials, with the ashes buried in upturned earthenware urns.

However we have little evidence of Bronze Age settlement in the area, although the burial sites and artefact finds across this part of Carmarthenshire show that there must have been a well-developed society here.

Two examples of Bronze Age '*burnt mounds*' have been recorded within the community, at Sarn Las and Blaenlliwe. These mounds of charcoal and burnt stone are thought to represent cooking hearths and suggests that people were settled nearby. Similar sites are found across Carmarthenshire, usually alongside a stream or river.

Archaeologists have excavated a number of Iron Age defended enclosures in the Llawhaden area, just to the west of Llanfallteg, and found that some of those sites had their origins in the Bronze Age. Similar defended enclosures are known locally, such as the enclosure underlying Llangan parish church, none of which have been excavated. It therefore remains to be seen if Bronze Age communities lived in such places.

The Iron Age

Around 2500 years ago, the influence of the Celtic world began to affect the area. The Iron Age is closely associated with the history of the Celts, who introduced iron weapons and tools. They are also the first people of this country to appear in historical sources, described by Roman and Greek authors.

Iron Age society was based on clans or tribal groups. Communities often lived in defended settlements, such as hillforts or defended enclosures. This is thought to reflect the fact that clan disputes and cattle raiding were endemic in Celtic society.

There are a number of defended enclosures dating from this period to be found in the parish. Individual examples are located at Cwmfelin Boeth and Blaenlliwe, two more at Henllan Farm, one close to Blaenwernddu Farm and another, perhaps the most significant, surrounding the church and churchyard at Llangan. This latter site consists of a series of concentric circles visible from the air as crop marks in dry periods.

The defended enclosures survive only as slight earthworks, but would have originally had substantial defences consisting of earth banks and ditches with timber palisade fences along the top of the banks. Inside would have been timber round houses and other structures. Smaller examples were probably Iron Age farmsteads, but larger defended enclosures, such as the one beside Llangan church, were the equivalent of the hillforts found in other areas.

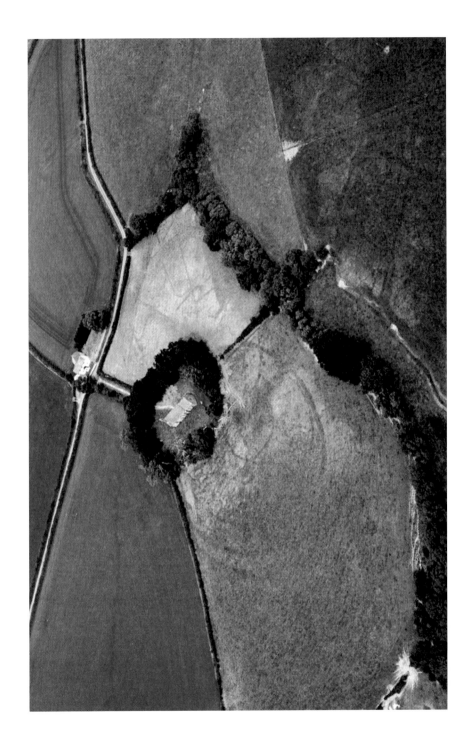

Llangan with cropmarks showing the early medieval village.
©Crown copyright; RCAHMW.

There are larger Iron Age hillforts in neighbouring communities. Just to the south, at Llanddewi Velfrey, are two examples known as Caerau Gaer and Llanddewi Gaer, both being Scheduled Ancient Monuments. An oval shaped hillfort has been found at Castell Pigyn at Llangan and also a heavily defended camp at Hafod, Llangan East in the parish of Llanboidy. Hafod Camp is also interesting historically as it is one of the few places in the area to yield evidence of Roman artefacts, indicating that the camp was still being used in Roman times.

It was first mentioned in 1811 by Richard Fenton in his book '*A Historical Tour through Pembroke*'

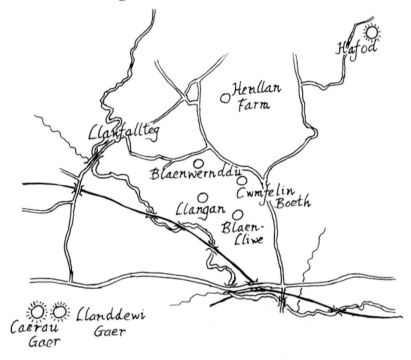

Map of enclosures and hillforts in area

The Roman Period

The invading Roman legions, under the leadership of Suetonius Paulinus, reached Wales in 48AD and began their campaign against the Celtic tribes of southern Wales. These were the Silures, who lived in the southeast of the country, and the Demetae who occupied the southwest. The Silures appear to have shown stiff resistance to the invaders, but it seems that in the southwest, the Roman advance met with much less opposition. Excavations of Iron Age sites in the region have not produced any evidence to show that hillforts and defended sites were destroyed by the legions. Indeed, it would seem that there was a relatively rapid and peaceful transition to a new order. A new centre of authority, administration and trade was established at Moridunum, in the heart of west Wales, the site of modern Carmarthen, which is the oldest settled town in Wales.

Around Llawhaden and Castell Henllys in Pembrokeshire, archaeologists have shown that the defended settlements were abandoned and new, undefended villages and farmsteads appeared alongside the old hillforts. By 78AD, the lands of the Demetae appear to have been fully under Roman control and the Romanisation of the country then commenced, leading to a prolonged period of peace and prosperity.

There are many examples of Roman coins and pottery being found within native defended settlements, which suggests that there was a trade between the native Celts and the Romans before and after the conquest period. The closest example to Llanfallteg is a single coin of the Emperor Domitian (81-96AD), which was found at Penbrwynen, Clynderwen and is currently kept at Tenby Museum.

In a number of locations, coins have also been found which may have been buried deliberately for safe-keeping. Three finds come from neighbouring communities. In 1800 some Roman coins were found at Hafod Camp, Llanboidy, which included coins from the time of the Roman Republic (c 82BC) up to the reign of Valens (364-378AD). Just to the north of Hafod Camp near Bronyscawen, is another fortification known as Y Gaer. Here, in 1692, two shepherds came across two leaden urns, which contained as many as 200 Roman coins, dating from the time of the Republic up to Vespasian (79AD). At Y Merydd, Cilymaenllwyd, an earthen vessel containing a large number of Roman coins was found, dating from the reigns of Commodus (172-192AD) to Severa (244-249).

In addition to these coin finds, we now know that a major Roman road was built west of Carmarthen and passed just to the south of

Llanfallteg. in which he describes visiting Glanrhyd and tracing its course through there and then through Park-yr-Eglwys, a field to the north of the Chapel of Castell Dwyran. Then it was generally known as Ffordd Helen or the Hywel Dda road, but it has also been known as the Via Julia. This however is an 18th century invention and not a genuine Roman name for the road.

Its existence was confirmed in the 1980s by crop marks seen on aerial photographs, and, prior to the construction of the Whitland bypass in 1987, a section of it was excavated at Pwll-y-Hwyaid Farm. Subsequent excavations at Bryn Farm, Llanddewi Velfrey, have revealed that the cobbled surface of the road was laid on top of a mound of shale clippings, clay and sand with a core foundation of large boulders. Linear cropmarks have shown that it extended to the south-west of Clynderwen, continuing west to Llawhaden and Wiston, where fragments of Roman amphorae (storage jars) have been found.

The Roman road near Whitland viewed from the west
(Cambrian Archaeology)

The Dark Ages

In 410AD, Roman Imperial authority was withdrawn from Britain, having lasted 350 years – a period of time equivalent to that between the reigns of Elizabeth 1 and the present Queen.

Even before the final departure of the Roman legions, the coasts of Britain had been subject to incursions from overseas. West Wales saw the arrival of immigrants from Ireland – a people called the Deisi. This tribe probably arrived initially as mercenaries, but they soon rose to positions of power and by the end of the 5th century AD they had founded Demetia, also referred to as the Kingdom of Dyfed.

The Deisi spoke Irish rather than the Brythonic language of the native Celts (which later developed into Welsh). Their writing, known as Ogam, consisted not of letters, but of straight strokes and notches and was used to record inscriptions on the edges of memorial stones. However, it is probable that Brythonic-speaking communities continued to live within the area throughout this period.

The first recorded ruler of the combined Kingdom of Dyfed, in the middle of the 5th century, was Tripun. He was followed by his son Aercol or Aergol Lawhir, who in turn was followed by his son Vortipore (or Vortiporix or Guotepir). He is commemorated by an inscribed stone which, (on the evidence of William Phillips and David Morgan, both in their seventies in 1895), originally stood on the south side of the stile giving access to the churchyard of Castell Dwyran near Llanfallteg.

Made of greenstone (the same stone as the altar stone at Stonehenge), it measures almost seven feet high, by two feet wide and one foot thick. The inscription is in both Latin and Ogam and reads *Memoria Voteporigis Protictoris*, which has been translated as *'the Memorial of Voteporix the Protector'*. There is also a wheel-cross inscribed on the front indicating that this was a Christian burial.

Castell Dwyran is reputed to be a foundation of great antiquity. In 1876 a programme of restoration was carried out, followed by rebuilding of the fence in 1879. The stone was then taken down and dragged to the side of a nearby hedge, on the right side of the lane that leads to Gwarmacwydd. It was left there until it was convenient for

Daniel, the Rector's workman to transport it to a field at Gwarmacwydd, where it was set up for use as a cattle rubbing post. At some stage it was whitewashed and, as the paint wore away from the raised surfaces over the years, the full extent of the inscription was revealed. In 1921, the then owner of Gwarmacwydd, Miss Bowen Jones, recognising the historical significance of the stone, donated it to Carmarthen Museum where it remains to this day.

Adjoining the northern bank of the churchyard at Castle Dwyran is a large field known as Parc-y-Eglwys already mentioned in connection with the Roman road. Tradition had it that, whilst it was permissible to plough that portion of the field furthest from the church, the piece next to it must not be broken up, else there will be *thunderings and lightnings and the cattle will die*. This part shows *signs of ancient foundations, apparently large hut circles, which could indicate that this is the site of the Castell, which gives the place its name*. Could this be where Vortipore lived and had his seat of power? Another significant indication is that it lies at the centre of the old Kingdom of Dyfed and very close to the route of the Roman road that would provide easy access to all parts of his realm.

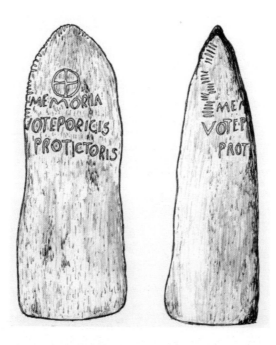

The Vortipore stone

As to Vortipore himself, he is mentioned by the 6th century monk and chronicler Gildas as '*The Tyrant of the Demetae, a bad son of a good father, a man who had grown grey hair in the service of the Devil and who shows no sign of repentance as he draws near his end.*' This certainly does not accord with the description of Protector on his monument but it should be noted that Gildas, in his treatise called '*De Excidio et Conquestu Britanniae*' ('*On the Fall and Conquest of Britain*'), was very critical of all the Welsh rulers, blaming their sinfulness for the disasters of the Anglo-Saxon invasions. However, hero or villain, Vortipore is certainly of great significance in the Llanfallteg area which, for ten years, could have held the seat of power for the whole of Dyfed in the mid 6th century.

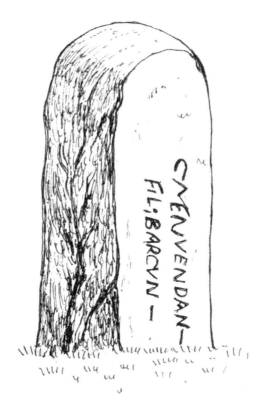

The Menvendanus stone

There is another fine example of an inscribed stone located locally. First recorded by Edward Lloyd in c. 1695, it was found lying in a field called Parc-y-main (*'The Field of the Stone'*) at Parke, Henllan Amgoed. It now stands in a field near the farm and is a scheduled ancient monument. It is known as the Menvendanus or Quenvendani Stone and the Latin inscription reads *'QUENVENDANI FILI BARCUNI'* which translates as `the body of Quenvendanus son of Barcunus'. There is some indication that it may have originally had an Ogam inscription along one edge, but that has now been eroded away. Nothing is known of the individuals mentioned other than that both are thought to have Irish names.

The Irish dynasty ruled over Demetia for several centuries, but the rise of the Welsh kingdom of Deheubarth in the early 10th century brought an end to Irish influence. Deheubarth was founded by Hywel Dda, who is famous for bringing together the leading lawmakers of his day around the year 930. They met at his hunting lodge on the banks of the Tâf, somewhere near modern Whitland (probably just outside Llanfallteg) to codify the Welsh laws.

The Laws of Hywel Dda provided an organised hierarchical model for Welsh society for centuries afterwards. The King was always the pinnacle of society, supported by a large number of court officials and servants. Beneath this ruling class, the population and land was divided into smaller units. The smallest unit was the *tref* or township. Four *tref* units made up a *maenor*, which was a small estate designed to be both self sufficient in the commodities required to maintain its population, and also produce a surplus to supply the ruling class. Each *maenor* would have a *llan* or church as its religious centre. Twelve *maenor* units, plus two extra *tref* units for the King formed a *cwmwd* or commote. Two commotes formed a *cantref*, which was the largest unit within a kingdom. By the time of Hywel Dda, the commote, because of its size, had become the most convenient division for the holding of the prince's court or *llys*, and for collecting the royal dues. The structure remained in place for several centuries.

We know that the Llanfallteg area fell within the commote of Amgoed, part of the cantref of Gwarthaf. It appears that many modern Welsh parishes and communities may well have their origins in these ancient divisions. Therefore, parishes such as Llanfallteg, Llangan and Henllan Amgoed, which were created in medieval times, may have been based on earlier *maenor* units for which we have no historic record.

Map of cantrefs and commotes

The Middle Ages

Wales developed into a battleground within a few years of William the Conqueror's victory over the English King Harold at Hastings in 1066. The Normans and Welsh fought continually over the next 200 years. William created a series of lordships along the length of the Welsh borders. These marcher lordships were virtually autonomous, with no defined boundaries on their Welsh sides, thus giving them leave to seize as much Welsh territory as they could. When Rhys ap Tewdwr, the ruler of Deheubarth, was killed near Brecon in 1093, Norman marcher lords began to make serious attempts to conquer southwest Wales. Undoubtedly, this area would have felt the impact

27

of military struggles that periodically raged across the region. Finally, the last Welsh prince of Deheubarth, Rhys ap Maredudd, was killed in 1292.

To establish their power bases, the marcher lords started by building castles, firstly simple motte and bailey constructions, but soon to be followed by massive structures of stone. The nearest stone castles to Llanfallteg are those at Llawhaden and Narberth. Smaller motte and bailey castles are found at Llanboidy and Lampeter Velfrey, but none are known within Llanfallteg itself.

Gerald of Wales

A 12th century figure, Gerald de Barri (known as Gerald of Wales), passed through the area. He was accompanying Baldwin, Archbishop of Canterbury, on a journey round Wales to secure volunteers and funds for the Third Crusade. According to Gerald's account of the journey, on Tuesday 22nd March 1188, they travelled from Whitland Abbey to Haverfordwest, crossing the River Tâf and the Cleddau near Llawhaden.

William de Breose and the Lordship of St Clears

The Norman Lordship of St Clears was formed by combining the ancient commotes of Amgoed and Peuliniog. Its exact boundaries are uncertain, but it filled the space between the Eastern Cleddau and Cynin rivers with the Tâf as its southern boundary. There is no definite evidence of a settlement at Llanfallteg prior to the coming of the Normans. Although the area would have been organised into *trefi* in accord with Welsh custom their names are long forgotten.

An early mention of St Clears came in 1152. In *Brut y Tywysogion* (The Chronicles of the Princes) we learn that, in that year, Rhys ap Gruffydd and a large force ravaged the castle of Ystrad Cyngen, which some believed to be the pre-Norman name for St Clears. It appears therefore, that there was a wooden castle at St Clears from the mid 12th century and the site, known as Banc y Beili, is still identifiable.

In 1195, St Clears was captured by the Marcher Lord William de Breose from Hywel Sais, son of the Lord Rhys. The de Breose family had been near neighbours of William the Conqueror in Normandy and fought in the Battle of Hastings.

At the start of King John's reign in 1199 his close friend and confidant William de Breose, the Earl of Bramber, was a successful but weary battle - hardened veteran. In 1202 de Breose helped John win a decisive victory at Mirabeau in France after the barons in Anjou-Pitou rebelled against John. In return, the King showered castles and land on de Breose, mainly in Wales, but also in Ireland and England.

After the 1202 campaign, William (1155-1211) withdrew from court and public life in favour of his son, the Lord of Brecon. By 1203, William was Lord of Gower, Radnor, Builth and upper Gwent. He also had strengthened his position in the Lordship of St Clears by acquiring the lands of the Devonshire magnate, John of Torrington. With the support of his grandsons, Rhys Ieuanc and Owain ap Griffudd, who were Lords of Deheubarth, de Breose was the most powerful lord in Wales.

William often neglected to pay his taxes during King John's reign, or negotiated a reduction. William refused to return to France when the French provinces rebelled again and the King began to regret giving him so many castles and estates. Matters came to a head in 1208 when King John demanded large sums of money from him in addition to much of his land. John's patience finally ran out with William and his wife Matilda de Valerys, when they refused to pay homage or to provide a suitable hostage.

It took two years and several military campaigns to displace de Breose, who fled to Ireland. In May 1210, John sent a large army along the coast roads of South Wales to Pembroke, crossing the ferries at Llanstephan and Laugharne on his way. King John found that Llewellyn Fawr had been plotting against him to help the fugitive de Breose regain his possessions and had persuaded the two young princes of Deheubarth, Rhys and Owain, to support him. To counter this, John met with a number of chieftains in South Wales and conferred privileges upon them in order to gain their support.

Matilda and her son then went to Scotland, where they were captured in 1210 and starved to death by King John. William disguised himself as a beggar and moved to France where he died in 1211. Their Welsh and Irish lands had been confiscated in 1208, although some were returned to the family many years later on payment of a large fee.

In 1215 Llewellyn Fawr made a surprise attack on the Normans in West Wales during a particularly mild December. Carmarthen was attacked on the 8th of that month and in turn Llanstephan, Laugharne and St Clears fell to him. On this last occasion, the castle at St Clears was burnt and utterly destroyed. As far as is known, it was never again fortified.

The de Breose lands that were confiscated by the Crown passed to William's daughters and these portions came to be known as Traynes, meaning thirds. William's daughter Maud married Roger Mortimer, Earl of March, so her's was eventually called Trayne March; Eve married William de Cantelope and her share of the land was passed on to William de Clinton, becoming known as Trayne Clinton. Elinor married Humphrey de Bohun, so her share of the land passed into the ownership of Morgan ap Maredudd to be called Trayne Morgan.

Trayne March consisted of the parishes of Llanboidy, Llanfallteg, Cilmaenllwyd and St Clears and contained the manors of Blaen y Merydd, Maenor Cilyllyn, Maenor Castell Dwyran and Maenor Mounton or Cilmaen.

Trayne Clinton had the parishes of Llangynin, Yr Hen Dy, Eglwys Llandre as well as parts of Llanfallteg and Cilmaenllwyd including the Manors of Bach Sulnew and Tredai.

Trayne Morgan also contained part of Llanfallteg together with the parishes of Henllan, Llangan, Llandysilio and Egremont. This included the manors of Tegfynydd, Henllan, Talfan, Egremont, Cilau, Pennycnwc, Castell Madoc, Clunty (or Glinty), Eithunduon and Dreinog. Most of these are identifiable today.

A list drawn up in 1275 for Edmund, Earl of Lancaster, of lands he controlled in Cardigan and Carmarthen, states that '*English*' lordships of St Clears, Laugharne, Llanstephan, the old Barony of Llawhaden, Cydweli, Carnwyllion and the Gower, together with the Welsh commotes of Elfed, Widigada and Derllys were under the control of Carmarthen Castle. When Rhys ap Gruffydd forfeited the lands of the Lordship of St Clears they passed into the eager hands of King Henry VIII.

The Battle of Cefnfarchen

In 1217 Llewelyn the Great of Gwynedd had marched south from his stronghold in Snowdonia to attack Southwest Wales and extend his territory. As he advanced westwards, the Flemings of Pembroke and Rhos, under the leadership of Wizo, marched to meet him to try and prevent him from attacking Haverfordwest. A battle took place, which Llewelyn won. The *'Chronicle of the Princes'* records that the two parties then met at a place called Cefn Cynfachen, which may be the same as the modern Cefnfarchen, and a peace treaty was negotiated. A field between Cefnfarchen and Parke known as Parc y Heddwch may have been the exact site where the peace talks were held.

The Black Death

Bubonic plague first arrived in Carmarthen in 1349, probably from infected rats on board the ships which plied the Severn estuary and which were in contact with English and Continental ports. Customs officers employed to check imported goods were amongst the first victims. The effects of the plague were devastating and it is estimated that between 30% and 50% of the town's population died.

Its occurance in 1361 and again in 1369 is mentioned in the records of Castell Dwyran church, suggesting that the Llanfallteg area was equally badly affected. The archives of the Bishop of St David's state that in 1563 there were 15 households in Llanfallteg, whereas in the prebendary of Llangan there were only two. In 1670 Llanfallteg had 13 hearth taxpayers and Llangan only two. Llangan appears to have been virtually wiped out by the Black Death and failed to revive.

The devastation is unimaginable now. Whole villages were abandoned with farmland reverting to waste, as there was no one left to work it.

The social effects were long lasting and it took three centuries for the population to return to its original level.

The plague returned again in the 17th century, with 300-400 people dying in Tenby, but there are no records of its effects in the Llanfallteg area. The High Constable issued a warrant preventing entry into, and exit from, Haverfordwest during an outbreak of plague in 1652. On the 13th May, Henry White and Samson Lort wrote to the High Constable requesting that the weighing and buying of wool, which usually took place in Haverfordwest, be held each week at Staunton on Tuesdays and Llawhaden on Saturdays.

The Post Medieval Period

The union of Wales and England was legally achieved by numerous acts of parliament between 1535 and 1545. The old marcher lordships were swept away and replaced by shires. English laws and county administration were extended to Wales. Twenty-four MPs were elected by the twelve Welsh shires and boroughs (Monmouth excluded), to represent Wales at Westminster. Local gentry and prominent businessmen, lawyers and men of learning now participated in the administration of the shires. The 1543 Act dictated that Welsh customs of tenure and inheritance were no longer permitted (they did in fact exist until the 18th century). The English language became the preferred tongue of commerce and local government organisations, although the populace of Llanfallteg would have noticed little difference.

By the 15th century the de Breose lands (most of Llanfallteg) had come under the control of Whitland Abbey. Virtually all the abbey lands, except the farms immediately adjacent to the abbey itself, were leased out and this continued with little change until the dissolution of the monasteries in 1539. There were 138 recorded leaseholders, mostly given for three generations and latterly 99 - year terms. As the leases expired, the land could be re-let or sold as the monarch decided. This resulted in existing landowners increasing their estate size, whilst copyholders and yeoman farmers suffered. Rents were increased, evictions and disputes became extremely common, and holdings and farms were frequently co-joined.

Despite the occurrence of the plague and failed harvests, the population of Wales had recovered to the level before the Black Death (two hundred and fifty years previously) at the death of Elizabeth I in 1603. Inflation was rife, unemployment was high, commodity prices doubled and wages in real terms halved, resulting in abject poverty for many. Landlords became wealthier by increasing rents and yeoman farmers wanted, and obtained, increased production. The peasantry had to work harder, and growing food at home was essential for survival.

These conditions created economic growth, in turn stimulating agricultural production and industry. The rich prospered and the new magnates often became landowners, through investing part of their wealth. James Hugh Lewes of Abernant Bychan (now Plas Glynarthen), Penbryn, was one prominent property owner and lessee in this area, who had land over a wide area of Ceredigion, near Pembroke and in Henllan Amgoed. He was granted a lease for 21 years on Abbey lands at Castell Cossan on 21st June 1594. James married twice; firstly Elizabeth Stedman of Ystrad Fflur and secondly Ann, daughter of John Wogan of Wiston. He served as High Sheriff of Cardiganshire in 1571 and 1589 and, as one of the five justices in the county, served in the livery of the Earl of Essex, who was a member of the Deveraux family.

It is during this time (1594) that he acquired considerable property in South Cardiganshire and numerous 21 - year Crown leases, particularly old abbey lands around Llanfallteg and the old abbey granges of Iscoed, Castell Cossan and half of Llanrhybyll. He died in 1598. In all probability, due to the family's standing, they would have applied to the Crown (Queen Elizabeth I) for the son to take over the leases. What actually happened is unclear. Searches through the Patent Roll, State Papers and the Court of Augmentations from 1600 onwards fail to identify any purchases or leases of lands. The court records of Elizabeth I are limited in comparison to those of Henry VII and Henry VIII. In all probability the Abbey lands passed from James Lewes to his son on payment of an appropriate fee, and were extended for a further 21 years, until 1629, in the reign of Charles I. The lands were probably sold at this time.

The crown sold off a considerable acreage, perhaps half of the grange areas, before 1645 to predominately, but not exclusively, Welsh families. The area north of Llanfallteg church was then in the ownership of the Matthias family.

Sources

Jones, F. *Historic Cardiganshire Homes and their Families*. Pages 8-9. Brawdy Books, 2000.

Laws, E. *Discovery of the tombstone of Vortipore, Prince of Demetia at Llanfallteg, Carmarthenshire. Archaeologia Cambrensis* series, 50: 303—307, 1895.

Caradog Llancarvan. *Brut y Tywysogion; Or, the Chronicle of the Princes of Wales*. Published by Adamant Media Corporation, 2001.

RELIGION

Early Christianity

Shortly before the fall of the Roman Empire, Christianity had become the Empire's only recognised religion. When the Romans withdrew in 410AD, Britain was predominantly a Christian country. During the following centuries, however, Christianity was weakened in the south and east of Britain, as power passed to pagan Anglo-Saxon rulers. The Christian church flourished in the Celtic north and west: Ireland, Scotland, Cornwall, Cumbria, and of course Wales.

Due to the strength and influence of the Christian church in the Celtic lands, the Dark Ages in Wales are often referred to as the '*Age of the Saints.*' During these centuries, Christian missionaries spread word of Celtic Christianity among the people, founding monastic communities and churches across the country. In about 600AD there was a papal order to Christianise sacred pagan sites. How his happened is unclear, as it may of involved the canonisation of local people or the construction of roofed wooden huts on the pagen sites.

Llangan church.
©Crown copyright; RCAHMW.

All the local churches are dedicated to Celtic saints: Henllan is dedicated to St David, Llanfallteg to St Mallteg and Llangan to St Canna. It is possible that the location of these churches were established religious places from the pre-Christian period, as some churches may have been built near sacred pagan sites, such as temples and wells.

The Saints

St David. The most prominent of these Celtic saints is, of course, St David or Dewi Sant, who was born in Pembrokeshire in the early sixth century. There are many churches throughout southern Wales dedicated to him, including that at Henllan Amgoed. St David was of noble birth, being the son of Sandde (brother of King Usai of Ceredigion) and Non, daughter of Lord Cynyr of Caer Goch in Pembrokeshire. It is believed that he was educated at Whitland by Saint Paulinus, who lived as a hermit. David travelled widely in Wales, Cornwall and Brittany, as well as to Jerusalem before founding a monastery at Glyn Rhosyn (later called St. David's) and becoming a bishop. He followed an ascetic life, was vegetarian and teetotal. He expected his followers to do likewise, push ploughs without draught animals and spend their evenings in prayer. St David died on 1st March 589.

St Mallteg. The saint celebrated in the dedication of the parish church at Llanfallteg is St Mallteg. Very little is known about this saint and there appear to be no other dedications to St Mallteg throughout the whole of Wales, but the name does appear on one of the most important early Christian monuments in Wales. The Cadfan Stone, at Tywyn church in Gwynedd, bears what is probably the oldest example of written Welsh in existence. It probably dates to 800AD or earlier, and has the following inscription:

+ CINGEN CELEN {*} TRICET NITANAM + TENGRUIN
MALTE(C) GUADGAN ANTERUNC DUBUT MARCIAU MOLT
{*} PETUAR M(C)ARTR

This translates as '*The body of Cingen lies beneath. Egryn, Mallteg, Gwaddian, together with Dyfod and Marchiau. The tomb...four. (--).* The appearance of the name Mallteg confirms that this personal name was in use during the Age of the Saints, although whether the Mallteg who appears to have been buried at Tywyn is the same person as St Mallteg we cannot say.

The Cadfan Stone

St Canna. In contrast, quite a lot is known about St Canna to whom the ancient church at Llangan is dedicated. She was a Breton princess who married Prince Sadwrn. They moved to South Wales, where they became Christians. Sadwrn left to become a hermit in Anglesey, so Canna remarried to Alltu Redegog. She later became a nun, founding churches in Llanganna and possibly Canton, as well as Llangan. Her main residence is said to have been here, where there is a holy well, Ffynnon Ganna, dedicated to her. A chair-shaped stone known as St Canna's Chair was, according to tradition, her seat. This is said to have been a stopping off - place for pilgrims travelling to St David's, where they sought respite and healing at her well. Her feast day is the 25th October.

For centuries Ffynnon Ganna was a place of pilgrimage in its own right for those suffering from agues or intestinal problems. The tradition was to throw pins into the well, drink from its water and then sit in the chair. If the patient managed to fall asleep in the chair then a cure was more likely. As recently as 1872 an old man remembered people undergoing treatment and he had seen hundreds of pins in the well. By 1840 the water level in the well had dropped as a result of the tenant carrying off soil between the well and the watercourse.

Canna's chair

Whitland Abbey

The establishment of Whitland Abbey was to have a significant effect on the economy of the wider district throughout the medieval period. During this time, the Cistercians had a vast network of abbeys across Europe around which some monks would travel, communicating ideas as they went. They were excellent farmers and their Welsh abbeys had a reputation for producing quality wool, much of which was exported to the Continent.

The Cistercian order of Monks was formed at Clairvaux in France in 1098. They believed in poverty, simplicity and separation from the material world. They wore coarse habits of undyed wool and were known as White Monks. Their lifestyle was rigid and based on agricultural labour and they chose remote locations for their abbeys, forcing them to be self-sufficient.

In 1140, Bernard, the first Norman Bishop of St David's, invited the Abbey of Clairvaux to send a colony of monks to Wales and by 1144 they were settled on land provided by him at Treffgarn, near Whitland. This settlement was only temporary however, and in 1151 they moved to their permanent site at Whitland, on land given by John Torrington, which they called Alba Landa and, later, Blanchland. The new abbey was carefully sited at the confluence of two rivers, the Gronw and the Colomendy, which enabled the monks to create an extensive complex of watercourses plus a mill and fishponds. These were vital to the economy of the community, which expanded rapidly, so that it may have eventually housed as many as one hundred monks. Its success led to the founding of seven daughter abbeys in Wales and one or two in Ireland.

Although its founder and first patrons were Normans, the Welsh soon began to join and patronize the new monastery, which, unlike the Benedictine monasteries, was an independent abbey. Before long it even had a Welsh abbot called Cynon and it is thought that the monks spoke in Welsh. It is therefore considered to be the first genuinely Welsh abbey. From about 1165 onwards, the Lord Rhys himself became its main patron and granted it much land. He even sent his son Maredydd, blinded as a child whilst a hostage of Henry II, to be a monk at Whitland.

Under the Lord Rhys, the community prospered and by the thirteenth century it had extensive landholdings organised around seventeen grange centres. Iscoed grange included the Abbey itself and extended as far west as Llanlliwe in Llangan. This grange was made up of scattered parcels of land, three of which fell partly or wholly within the modern community of Llanfallteg. Castell Cossan grange was north of the abbey in what is now Llanboidy. There was also a grange, possibly called Llwynrebol, in Llandisilio East. The exact areas of each of the granges are uncertain as the abbey records were destroyed at the dissolution. It is also unclear just when the lands within or surrounding the parishes of Llanfallteg became part of the Whitland Abbey granges. The lost records would have told us when the land was gifted to them and by whom, as well as its area and boundaries. They would also have shown how, in the very last part of the thirteenth century, abbey lands were leased out to individuals who in turn sub - let them as they thought fit - the granges in effect becoming manors. At the dissolution there were 133 leases on more than 20,000 acres of abbey lands equating to something like 1000 to 1500 tenants (a deduced figure, possibly on the low side).

The dissolution of the monasteries brought about the closure of Whitland Abbey. In 1536 the abbot, William ap Thomas, paid the vast sum of £400 to keep the abbey open but it survived only three more years, finally closing in 1539 when only five monks remained. The abbey and its estates passed to the Crown. After this happened, a succession of monarchs leased out or sold off the lands whenever and to whoever they could, until the reign of Charles 1 (1625-1649).

Another important ecclesiastical and administrative centre was found at Llawhaden. This barony had been gifted to the Bishops of St David's. Llanfallteg church and lands close to the modern village formed a small grange or manor in the possession of the Bishop of St David's, who had his own granges across Pembrokeshire and Carmarthenshire. The place name Rhyd-ddol-esgob in Llanfallteg is possibly an echo of this ancient connection with the bishops.

Churches and Chapels

There are three parish churches in the modern community, due to the 1930 restructuring of the parish boundaries that combined Henllan

Amgoed with Llanfallteg West & East, along with part of Llangan. A fourth church, Castell Dwyran, lies just outside the parish. All are now disused. Four chapels built by different non-conformist denominations complement these churches.

The local churches and chapels are:

- *Llangan parish church dedicated to St Canna*
- *Llanfallteg parish church dedicated to St Mallteg*
- *Henllan Amgoed parish church dedicated to St David*
- *Castell Dwyrain chapel of ease*
- *Congregationalist chapel in Henllan Amgoed*
- *Capel Mair in Llanfallteg*
- *Bethania Methodist chapel in Cwmfelin Boeth*
- *Capel Rhos in Llanfallteg*

In our secular age it is unlikely that we can understand the importance that superstition, belief and religion had in the lives of our forebears. Only a hundred years ago the population supported eight churches, but now only the chapel in Henllan Amgoed holds regular services, although there is still an occasional service at Capel Mair.

Churches

Medieval churches were the centres of the community; the chancel containing the altar was sacred, but the nave was used for a number of non-religious functions. Courts might be held, and tenants paid their rents in the church. Local medieval officials included the reeve, *maer* in Welsh. Beadles summoned tenants to the Manorial Court.

The key lay official after the Reformation was the Churchwarden, who represented the laity and safeguarded the valuables. An example of another duty is the '*bastardy bond*' of £50 for the maintenance of the bastard child or children of singlewoman Esther Morris of Llangan, given to the Churchwarden to administrate in April 1807 by three local yeomen. Illegitimacy was a social disgrace.

Because of the relative poverty of the parishes, the clergy often served several churches at once so they could have a reasonable income, and often there was no vicarage or glebe (land) for them to live in.

The earliest records of ministers are from around 1400. The Bishop of St David's, Guy de Mone, appointed William Mone to *Llanveylheg* church in 1398 and Roger Orchard followed him in 1399. It is possible that William Mone was a relative of the Bishop and his appointment was nepotic. Their contemporaries at Henllan Amgoed church were William Merry and John Wythe who took over in 1404. John Bell was vicar of Castell Dwyran in 1492, whilst William Wilcox was vicar in '*interesting times*,' as he was appointed in 1535, just in time to see the Dissolution of the Monasteries.

The records also show the Welsh patronymic naming system. When John Cradog became vicar of Henllan Amgoed in 1491 the names of the freeholders in the village were Rhys ap Phillip, Phillip ap Meredith ap Hoel, Rhys ap Hoel ap Rees, Rhys ap Llewelin ap David, Owen ap Howell ap Ros, Nest daughter of Llewelin ap David and Philip ap David Vaughan, tutor and guardian of sons and heirs of Owen ap Gruffith ap David ap Owen.

Pilgrims travelling to St David's would have passed close by, probably staying overnight at Whitland Abbey before taking the old Roman road west through Llawhaden and on to Wiston. Almost certainly they would have stopped at Llangan to visit St Canna's well and chair, and also possibly at Castell Dwyran, which was very close to the Roman road.

Llangan was an important church for many years; there is a seat reserved in St David's Cathedral for the prebendary of Llangan. This was a privilege not afforded to any other local church, including Llanboidy or Whitland. William Attwater resigned as prebendary of Llangan in 1514 to become Bishop of Lincoln. Lincoln Cathedral with a spire of 525 feet was, at the time, the tallest building in the world.

Llanfallteg Church

The churchyard may have been a religious site since pre-Christian times, and the church has been rebuilt a number of times over the centuries. The present church was rebuilt around 1800 and restored later in the century. It was built with limestone rubble, with yellow oolitic limestone round all the openings. There is a single bellcote. Like the other local churches, it is small, was rebuilt during the Victorian period and is now empty and disused, although the cemeteries have occasional burials.

Llanfallteg church is dedicated to St Mallteg and it appears to have always been in the possession and diocese of the Bishops of St David's. Thomas Morgan in 1707 stated that there were 36 families in the parish, that there were normally 12 communicants and that the sacrament was administered four times per year.

A 1710, a report about a visit by the Archbishop of Carmarthen to Llanfallteg stated: '*The vicar, Thomas Morgan, is also vicar of Llanddewi Velfrey and Crino and also Archdeacon of Carmarthen he holds two sermons every month at Llanfallteg, one in Welsh and the other in English. There are two families of dissenters, one of Quakers and the other of Ano Baptists. There were 30 communicants of the 60 families attending the Easter sacrament of bread and wine*'

The church was in a poor state with an ash tree growing out of the east wall of the chancel, the church and chancel walls needed rendering; the floor was uneven and unpaved and none of the windows were glazed.

Nor were the other churches in a better state, Llangan shared a Minister with Castell Dwyran, Cilymaenllwyd and Eglwys Fair Lan

Tâf (Whitland). All of them were reported as having uneven floors and unglazed windows.

All the Ministers stated that most parishioners went to the '*Meeting in Chapel*' as well as to Church.

Non-conformism

The Protestant reformers, who emerged as part of the Reformation in Europe during the 16th century, attacked numerous aspects of the Roman Catholic Church. Those included devotion to saints and the Virgin Mary, the concept of purgatory, celibacy of the clergy, the sacraments, Papal authority and corruption.

The year 1547 saw new injunctions to clergy who were issued with specimen sermons and instructed to remove images and shrines. Jewels and plate were confiscated. The church had to be cleared of any catholic ritual or decorative accoutrements. The previously vivid coloured interiors became whitewashed, preaching *per se* was banned and replaced by readings from the official homilies. English was predominately used by the church as well as Latin. The official bible remained in Latin, and two approved English versions appeared in 1536 and 1539 but nothing in Welsh. King Edward VI came to the throne in 1547 at nine years of age and has been described as precocious and bigoted, and became a staunch Protestant. Following the Acts of Uniformity 1549 and 1552 the Books of Common Prayer was introduced in English.

The Protestants, or Puritans, urged '*purity*' in doctrine and morality. They dispensed with the hierarchy of bishops, so elders within the congregation made decisions. Many remained within the Church of England, advocating that reformation needed to continue. Others believed that the Church was too corrupt for true Christians; these separatists were known as dissenters after the restoration of the monarchy in 1660, whilst those that remained in the Church were referred to as non-conformists for not conforming to the Book of Common Prayer.

There is a record of some local religious protests: Richard Parry of Penderi had a reputation as an '*uncontrollable brawler and barrater, alien from the Puritan ideal*' and was imprisoned in 1634 for not paying a fine. In 1637, Dorothy Price, the wife of Arthur Wogan, was charged with recusancy (not complying with the Established Church).

The area (like most of Wales) was largely Royalist during the Civil War; the '*anti-Puritan*' clergy were ejected in February 1649 from Llangan, Henllan Amgoed and Llanfallteg. In 1654 the commission for approbation of public preachers – '*The Triers*' - was established to fill vacancies with Puritan Ministers: Morgan Rice was appointed as rector of Llanfallteg, Jon Rice to Henllan and Thomas Jones to Llangan. Thomas Jones' tenure was initially brief; he was sequested in 1650 for '*drunkenness and malignancy*' but he was restored to his post in 1657.

The Anglican Church has always been a broad church, ranging from the neo-Catholics of the High Church to the non-conformists in the Low Church (although the words High and Low Church were not in common parlance then). Dissenters formed several denominations, especially after the Act of Toleration of 1689 made it legal to worship outside the Church of England. The Quakers however were persecuted. A law passed in 1662 made it illegal for them to hold services, and many spent time in gaol as a result. Quakers met illegally in private houses, until a meeting house was built near Narberth. There were certainly Quakers in the village in 1710, although many in the local area had left for America by this time. There is a Quaker burial ground at Trewern, which is just across the River Tâf from Penderi.

Henllan Amgoed Chapel

Non-conformism in Wales started during the 17th century. Initially people met in secret to avoid persecution, either outside or in places like *yr ystafell dywyll* ('*the dark, windowless room*') at Canerw in Llanboidy. Carnew was associated with the ministry of Stephen Hughes, who was known as *Apostol Sir Gaerfyrddin* ('*the Apostle of Carmarthenshire*'). Stephen Hughes (1622-1688) was one of the leading ministers of the time and he encouraged congregations during this time of persecution.

Religious persecution reduced dramatically after the accession of William and Mary and the Act of Toleration of 1689 allowed non-conformists to have their own ministers and build meeting houses.

Henllan Chapel

David John Owen of Llangan, Evan John Owen of Kiffig, John David Lewis of Eglwys Fair a Churig and Lewis Pryddroe of Egremont *'being four actual members of the congregation of dissenting protestants that were and are wont to meet for the performing of religious worship and divine service in the several and respective places of Pale, Canerw and Egrement in the aforesaid county'* acquired land in 1695 for the building of a meeting house. Palmawr in Cyffig was a meeting point that had been active from around 1650. In 1696, the householder died. The congregation split, some went to Laugharne, the rest attended meetings at Cefnfarchen farmhouse in Llanfallteg before Henllan Chapel was completed in 1697. Henllan Chapel was rebuilt and enlarged three times in 1724, 1777 and 1831 to hold the expanding congregation. The last major renovation was in 1924. It was one of the earliest chapels in the area, and dominated local religion until the present day.

When Henllan Chapel was built, it was estimated that only 2% of the worshipping population in Wales were non-conformists, indeed there were only two non-conformist families in Llanfallteg in 1710 (one of Quakers, the other of Anabaptists). But the growth was dramatic, by the time of the Battle of Waterloo (1815), a third of worshippers were non-conformists, and by 1851 the figure was 80%.

Most Protestants in Britain followed doctrine based on the views of John Calvin (1509-1564), which included the concepts of predestination and that people were '*depraved*' and needed to be saved from original sin by being '*elected*' by God to join the Church. The views of Jacobus Arminius (1560-1609) were a cornerstone of Methodism: he rejected predestination and believed in univeral salvation (all can be '*saved*').

The differences between Wesleyan (Methodist) and Calvinist thought resulted in several schisms in the congregation at Henllan Amgoed, most noticably between 1707 - 1709. This ended in the ejection of Lewis Thomas and his Calvinist supporters, who founded a new congregation at Rhyd-y-ceisiaid. A second schism in 1711 saw a group led by Mathias Maurice and Henry Palmer moving to Rhyd-y-ceisiaid. Henry Palmer, who was a local farmer, then returned in 1721 to be ordained minister at Henllan Amgoed.

Nathaniel Rowland (1749-1831) married Margaret Davies and they lived at Parke in Henllan Amgoed, which she inherited from her father. He became secretary of the Calvinist Methodist Association and had charge of the Tabernacle chapel in Haverfordwest. He had a reputation for arrogance and being domineering with his congregation. In 1807 he was excommunicated for drunkenness at the Newcastle Emlyn Association. He is buried at Henllan Amgoed.

In 1851 there were 550 in the congregation, with 145 scholars in the afternoon. Joshua Lewis, the minister, stated '*the congregation is not very fluctuating and the difference will be very little next Sunday or the following*'.

Religion can be an enormously divisive issue in any community and although tensions over the centuries reduced, friction can be detected in some of the church and school records as more and more people switched their allegiance from the Church of England to the chapels. A report on St. Dewi's in 1710 stated '*most of the Parishioners that come to Church go sometimes to the Meeting: but were the Minister's Duty perform'd as it ought to be, 'tis to be hop'd that the numbers of Dissenters might decrease*'.

The Llanfallteg school logbook has the following entries:

- *10th August 1897 – School closed. Meetings in Henllan in memory of 200 years of the church*

- *23rd April 1906 – There is a section of the people of this neighbourhood prejudiced against this school and have sent their children to Henllan.*

- *11th September 1906 –three more have left for Henllan*

- *11th July 1909 – the two children who lately quitted this school had not been punished and were on good terms when I last saw them. I have been given to understand that they had intended to leave after the Inspector's visit. The current denominational feeling is too powerful for me in this locality. All members of the Capel Mair Chapel have removed their children except two babies living near the school and could not go elsewhere. There is only one senior boy who is very delicate and could not go to a further school.*

Capel Mair

Capel Mair was built about 1878 to save the walk to Henllan Amgoed chapel. Evan and Mari Thomas of Rhydtirdu started Sunday schools in their home, one for boys and the other for girls in a different room. Later a choir was established. In 1876 plans to build a chapel in Llanfallteg were formulated. Mari Thomas then donated the land to build the chapel and she placed 50 gold sovereigns on the foundation stone to start the building. The chapel is still open, but only holds a couple of services a year.

Willie Reynolds outside Capel Mair

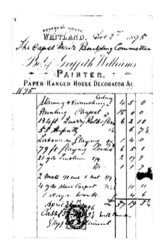

Capel Mair building committee receipt

Bethania, Cwmfelin Boeth

Two Methodist families in Llangan, the Jones of Talfan and Howell
Davies of Ysgubor Newydd, began Methodist services in 1842. They
were held in various houses in the neighbourhood, along with a
Sunday School in W. Scourfield's workshop in Cwmfelin Boeth.
Building a chapel was discussed for several years, but '*it was on the
border of two counties and one county looking at each other*'. Howell
Davies bought a small piece of land in 1859, which he offered for use
as a chapel and graveyard. Building began the following year and
Bethania Chapel was opened on 13th August 1861. Services continued
for a century, although the congregation was never large.

Capel Rhos

Baptists believe that the church should be made up of believers, not
just everybody who lived in the vicinity. They only support the
baptism of '*believers*', so children are not baptised as they are thought
too young to understand.

The Baptists in Llanfallteg held services in the smithy at Ty Newydd,
but in 1914 they started to discuss building their own chapel to save
the walk to chapel in Login, Blaenconin Chapel in Llandissilio or
Ffynnon Chapel in Llanddewi Velfrey.

Capel Rhos in 2009

Construction started in 1914 on some land left by Evan John of Llanfallteg House. Mr Price, a mason, built the chapel, which was opened in 1915 with a service held on the bank of the Tâf opposite the chapel for the 64 members. Originally the chapel was referred to as Capel Bach and Capel Ifan. The chapel closed in 1978.

Tithes

Traditionally, parishioners paid 10% of their income as a tithe to support the church. This was to be spent on the parish priest, the fabric of the church, the bishop and the poor. This meant handing over a tenth (the word tithe literally means a tenth part) of their yearly production of corn, hay, wool and other produce. Not surprisingly, tithes were unpopular. Many agreed with John Selden: *'tis ridiculous to say the Tythes is God's part and therefore the clergy must have them'*.

When the monasteries were dissolved in the 16th century, much church property, including the rights to tithe, passed into the hands of private individuals or *'Lay Impropriators'*. Over time more land across England and Wales was enclosed and many tithe owners were compensated by allotments of land. In some areas tithe payments in kind were converted to money payments, by agreement between local churchmen and landowners and occupiers.

The Tithe Commutation Act of 1836 converted tithes throughout the country from payments in kind to monetary payments. Tithe maps and apportionments made under the 1836 Act give us a picture of rural life in Llanfallteg in the middle of the 19th century.

By the mid-nineteenth century, many non-conformists were refusing to pay their tithes, as they did not attend the parish churches. As a result the old churches were often in a poor state, having stood for centuries. They required regular repair and were usually rebuilt more than once, many during the Victorian era.

There was local unrest about tithe payments; one rebel was Thomas Jones who farmed at Wernlygoes. A report entitled '*the Tithe Agitation*' in The Times on 28th January 1888 stated '*In the parish of Llanfallteg, Whitland, tithe distress sales began yesterday, and will be continued next week. The first sale took place on the farm of Mr. T. Jones, a leading Nonconformist, who had resisted all the tithe rent-charges for the past two years. The amount of tithe owing was about £17, for a rick of hay and three stacks of corn had been seized by the authorities. The auctioneer and bailiff were accompanied by a strong force of police under the command of Chief Constable Phillips, Major Bates, and Captain Scott. On approaching the farm they were surrounded by a crowd of six or seven hundred people, who hooted and yelled at them. Mr. Arthur J. Williams M.P., the Rev. Aaron Williams, the Rev. William Thomas, and Mr. Thomas Williams J.P. (who attended as a deputation from the Welsh Liberal Federation), stepped forward and entreated the crowd to fall back. The people eventually yielded and the farm-yard was reached. Here a large effigy of the rector of the parish in full canonicals was fixed on the top of a stack of corn. Large hoardings with Welsh mottoes were also erected. The bidding started at £5, but the rick was ultimately knocked down at £18, amid much jeering, and the constabulary subsequently withdrew. An indignation meeting was afterwards addressed by Mr. A. Williams M.P., and several Nonconformist ministers.*'

Sources

www. Genuki.org.uk

Henllan Amgoed Independent Church, Chapel Archives

John, T & Rees, M. *Pilgrimage, A Welsh Perspective*. Gomer, 2002.

Jones, E.W. *Braslun o Hanes Capel Mair Llanfallteg*, 1978.

Jones, F. *The Holy Wells of Wales*. Cardiff University Press, 1954.

Lewis, E. T., *Local Heritage from Efailwen to Whitland* ,1975.

Lewis, S. *A Topographical Dictionary of Wales,* 1844.

Lloyd, Sir John E., (Ed.). *A History of Carmarthenshire 2 vols.,* Cardiff, London Carmarthenshire Society, 1935, 1939.

Rowlands, J & S (Ed.) *Welsh Family History – A Guide to Research 2nd edition*, 1998.

Williams, G. *The Welsh Church from Conquest to Reformation*. University of Wales Press Cardiff, 1962.

EDUCATION

Llangan appears to have opened the earliest school in our area. In 1711, four poor children were taught in the Church, at the expense of the Minister, and by 1756 the numbers being taught had risen to 94.

Circulating schools

Griffith Jones, rector of Llanddowror near St Clears, set up a system of circulating schools. In 1730 he taught two young men to read and then sent them out to set up classes in barns, cottages and church buildings. The pupils, in turn, set up other classes. Griffith Jones instructed his teachers at *Yr Hen Goleg* (The Old College) in Llandowror before they were sent out into the countryside. By the time of his death in 1761, 3000 of these classes had been set up and 13 years later the number had passed 6000. Each class lasted a few weeks and attracted people of all ages. When the circulating schools started, reading and arithmetic classes were held at St Canna's Church as well as at other venues, including Llwyncelyn, Hiraeth, Blaenhiraeth and Rhyd-ddol-esgob.

Llanfallteg's first school was established at Wernlygoes in 1844. The master was described as an excessively ignorant man. He had been employed in this type of school via Madam Bevan's Charity for four years. The premises were rented free by a tenant of the farm '*the room was partly mud walled, thatched and open roofed, the floor of bare earth and very uneven.*' A Sunday school was held there. Samuel Lewis in his Topographical Dictionary of Wales writes that: '*there were 2 day schools and 55 children instructed at the expense of their parents.*'

Yr Ysgol Goch (The Red School) was the National School (Anglican as opposed to Nonconformist), and the first school in the village. It was open from 1869 to 1897. The Gower family donated the land, which was at the northern end of Brickyard Moor. The rector of Llanfallteg, Thomas Evans who lived at Lan, built the school at his own expense. When it closed in 1897 the pupils transferred to the county council Board School opposite on the Penybont fields.

Low attendance marred the life of the Attendance Officer and he habitually called at the homes of the children who were constantly absent. Time off from school was generously given to attend ploughing matches, haymaking, agricultural shows, local farm sales, the pleasure fair, public meetings, temperance meetings, potato digging and jumble sales.

Influenza absented pupils in January 1898 and in 1899 scarlet fever and diphtheria cases spiralled, followed by measles. School had to close for a short time with an epidemic of mumps in 1911. Skin diseases were prevalent, probably due to lack of cleanliness. Measles, again, was prevalent in 1915. At the same time there was an outbreak of face and scalp sores, and after verification, the school nurse closed the school for a month. Scarlet fever, diphtheria and whooping cough re-appeared in 1917 at epidemic proportions. The visiting Nurse Parish in June 1920 reported that '*some of the girls were not very clean*'. Any outbreak of illness was hard to confine due to the living conditions and lack of modern day drugs.

The school lacked a toilet; in the logbook there are a number of requests to have one supplied. Eventually, in 1921, temporary zinc closets were delivered to the school by motor lorry '*but had not been fixed for use*'.

Llanfallteg School

Problems in keeping pupils warm were constant through the winter months. In December 1897, there is an entry '*work all done on slate this morning due to the weather being so cold*'. The ink must have been frozen in the inkwells. In October 1919, there was a rail strike and no coal was available. It was bitterly cold in school and eventually in November 3 cwt of anthracite (a hundredweight, cwt, is 50 kilgrammes) was delivered to the school from C. Evans of Llanfallteg and 15 cwt of house coal arrived from H. Morris of Clynderwen. In December 1920 a hard frost interfered with schoolwork and the desks were moved as close as possible to the fire. The temperature was 36 degrees Fahrenheit (3° Celsius) and had been so for four days. In February 1921 the coal in the coalhouse was riddled and the dust sold to the local blacksmith.

The two large houses in the area, Tegfynydd and Glanrhyd are frequently mentioned in the logbooks. A request from Mrs Walker of Tegfynydd on the 23rd November 1915, that the schoolchildren should welcome a group of injured Australian soldiers at the Railway Station, was approved and the children 'marched' to the station. Tegfynydd sometimes held tea parties for the pupils. A number of entries through the years state that the pupils were 'marched' to Glanrhyd, a very historical place, also the old Church at Castell Dwyran and part of the old Roman road. It appears that although the Roman road was not greatly advertised, it was well known to the local inhabitants.

In the early 20th century, small rural schools made a concerted attempt to force the pupils to speak only English and anyone caught speaking their mother tongue in the confines of the school was made to wear a wooden tablet round their neck; the tablet was inscribed WN – Welsh Not (to be spoken). This was passed from child to child during the day and the poor soul who was left wearing it was caned the following morning.

In 1906 the school hit the headlines when the school governors decided that lessons should be bilingual, but, in August 1908, the logbook states that Welsh could not be taught as well as possible until the new textbooks arrived. Due to the decision to teach in Welsh and English, a section of the people in the neighbourhood became prejudiced against the school and began moving their children to Henllan School.

Llanfallteg School closed down on Friday 12th September 1958 and the pupils transferred to Henllan School. The building was used for many years by George Adams, a corn merchant from Tâf Alaw opposite as a store. It is still standing, empty and privately owned.

1. Jimmy John, Glanrhyd.	13. Liz Adams, 2 Adams Row.
2. Vivian Edwards, Station House.	14. Enid Adams, 2 Adams Row.
3. Hayden Davies, Ty-bach.	15. Nell Reynolds, Pen-y-bont.
4. Jack Beynon, Cross Farm.	16. Maggie James, 1 Adams Row.
5. Ronald John, Glanrhyd.	17. Glyn Griffiths, College Farm.
6. Tommy Evans, Wern-las.	18. Sydney John, Glanrhyd.
7. Tommy Davies, Maes-y-felin.	19. Nelly James, 1 Adams Row.
8. Ivor Morris, Head Teacher.	20. Ruby John, Glanrhyd.
9. Benyon Davies, Ty-bach.	21. Evelyn Adams, 2 Adams Row.
10. Mary Thomas, Tegfynydd Mill.	22. Irene Morris, 1 Glen View.
11. Maggie Jenkins, Maen-llwyd.	23. May Thomas, Plas-parce.
12. Dylis Adams, 2 Adams Row.	24. Bessie John, Allt-fach.

Llanfallteg school pupils in 1923

1. Alcwyn Owen, Felin Bryn.	17. Peggy Morgan, Taf Cottage.	33. Stella Morris, Glen View.
2. Ivor Owen, Pant-y-maen.	18. Dorris Thomas, Spring Gardens.	34. Cecil Edwards, Station House.
3. Ronald John, Glanrhyd.	19. Dylis Adams, 2, Adams Row.	35. Nancy James, 1 Adams Row.
4. Ronnie Morgan, Taf Cottage.	20. Mary Thomas, Tegfynydd Mill.	36. Hugh Morgan, Compton House.
5. Kenneth Morgan, Taf Cottage.	21. Evelyn Adams, 2 Adams Row.	37. Nell Reynolds, Pen-y-bont.
6. Morgan Nicholas, Llanfallteg Farm.	22. Parry Morgan, Compton House.	38. Lloyd Jenkins, Maenllwyd.
7. David Morgan, Compton House.	23. Mary Nicholas, Llanfallteg Farm.	39. Vivian Edwards, Station House.
8. Sal Morris, Taf Cottage	24. Ivor Webb, Rhyd-dol-esgob.	40. Jimmy John, Glanrhyd.
9. Nesta Nicholas, Llanfallteg Farm.	25. Lena Edwards, Station House.	41. Tom Thomas, Plas-parce
10. David Morgan, Compton House.	26. Eirwen John, Allt-fach.	42. Hayden Davies, Ty-bach.
11. Gwyneth John, Fron-haul.	27. May Jenkins, Maenllwyd	43. Willie John, Glanrhyd.
12. Bettie John, Castle Dwyran.	28. Gwen Thomas, Plas-parc.	44. Gordon Phillips, Post Office.
13. Averill Morris, Taf Side.	29. Bessie John, Allt-fach.	45. William Reynolds. Pen-y-bont.
14. Vernon Thomas, Tegfynydd.	30. Maggie Jenkins, Maenllwyd.	46. Ivor Morris, Head Teacher.
15. Barbara Thomas, Tegfynydd.	31. Maggie Davies, Allt-y-pistyll.	
16. Peggy Reynolds, Pen-y-bont.	32. Douglas Phillips, Hope Cottage.	

Llanfallteg school pupils in 1926

Teacher -   Miss Dilys Eynon

Standing -   Robert Davies; Alwyn Bowen; Anthony Rees; Ida Butler; Eileen Price; Darryl Davies; Marwen Bowen

Seated -   Selwyn Price; Kay Rees; Rebecca Morgan; Myfanwy Price; Ann Rees; Geraint Bowen.

Llanfallteg school pupils in 1958
(Pauline Griffiths, Wilson Museum Narberth)

Henllan Amgoed School

The Aberbanc National School was opened at Henllan Amgoed in 1848, teaching children between the ages of 5 and 11 years. It followed an earlier school, established at Henllan Independent Chapel in 1842, where the master's income was £25. 0s. 0d. per annum. The earliest school in this area was in 1720. In 1739 the local vicar cruelly reported that '*a poor mangy person taught at the school but most of his scholars are poor men's children.*'

Much information on the lives of villagers can be gleaned from the logbooks. In September 1898 after two month's holiday the school reopened, having had new furnishings and the mud floor levelled and blocked. To celebrate the opening of this '*new room*', a tea party was given in the afternoon and an evening meeting held, where former students gave a vivid account of their earlier years at the school.

In 1928 the dentist, M Griffiths and his nurse visited the school for the purpose of tooth extractions. In 1964 the dentist was unable to extract pupils' decayed teeth, as no gas was available.

The local Education Officer began to focus on pupil's health and well being and in 1935 the free milk scheme was set up to give each poor child 1/3rd of a pint every day. A local farmer, Mr Williams of Llwynderw, supplied milk to Henllan Amgoed School in bulk and the staff at the school had to share it out. Then in 1937, 55 pupils had the opportunity to have Horlicks in their dinner hour and 36 decided to do so. For many years the schools had allowed children to bring in cans of tea which would be left heating on the classroom stove. School meals commenced in 1948, conveyed in containers from Ffynnonwen and by 1954, a cook and assistant prepared meals for the children in school. In the event of a power cut, the cook used the stove of Mrs. Nicholas living opposite to the school, to prepare the meals.

Pupils who came long distances to Henllan Amgoed School were issued with wellington boots in 1944. The bad winter of 1947 hit most of the UK and Henllan Amgoed and Llanfallteg did not escape. In February and March all roads to the school were blocked and closed and the few children appearing in school were promptly returned home. Again in 1963, with the cold weather, the water pipes remained frozen in the school for a month and so the school was closed during this time.

During the First World War, Henllan Amgoed School took an active part in collecting funds. A patriotic concert for the Carmarthenshire Battalion and YMCA War Fund took place in May 1915 and the Head attended a conference on the War Savings Association for which the school had a day off. Another holiday was given in 1918 for the cessation of hostilities.

When the Second World War commenced, Air Raid Precautions instruction was given to the School Head at Carmarthen, and staff were given time off enabling them to assist in voluntary work. Pupils were also given safety-first lectures. Evacuation began in 1940 and Henllan Amgoed received some of these children into school. During

Wings for Victory Week, in 1943, the school raised the amazing amount of £1214. 12s. 6d. Their target had been £150. The total sum raised in 1944 for Salute the Soldier Week was over £400. In 1945 the school closed for VE Day (Victory in Europe) celebrations and at the end of June the last evacuee returned home.

Electric power and lighting was installed in the school in September 1955. The school had a telephone on 1st January 1971, the number being 565. The first Xerox 1030 photocopier arrived in 1989.

Henllan Amgoed School

Over the years, Henllan Amgoed School's registration increased steadily. In 1903 there were 94 on the register but by 1906 the numbers had increased to 107. Eventually when Llanfallteg School closed in September 1958 the 13 pupils transferred to Henllan, Efailwen, Brynconin, Narberth and Llanddewi Velfrey schools. In 2004, the National Assembly gave notice to close Henllan Amgoed School and the pupils were transferred to Ysgol Bro Brynach, a new area school in Llanboidy. For the first time in almost 300 years there is no school in the Henllanfallteg community.

Sources

School log books

Lewis, E. T. *Local Heritage from Efailwen to Whitland* , 1975.

Shepherd, Alan. *Visitors Going to Pembrokeshire*

Memories 1835 to 2004 Ysgol Henllan Amgoed.

TRACKS AND ROADS

From early times, tracks were made along the most convenient routes between two points. As the population grew the traffic became heavier. Carriages, carts, horses and livestock made the trackways wider and muddier. At times, especially in the winter, they were impassable.

A Roman road runs west from above the Whitland bypass past Penback and Sarn Las (*sarn* means '*causeway*' or '*paved way*'), where it crosses the Tâf, then runs to the north of Bryn Farm and onto Glanrhyd and Castell Dwyran. From there the road continues to Clynderwen and Llawhaden. There is some evidence that there was a road here before the arrival of the Romans, who simply may have improved an existing track. Certainly, this route was important for centuries, and would have been used by many people, including pilgrims travelling between Whitland and St David's.

In 1555 during Queen Mary's reign, the upkeep of the roads became the responsibility of each Parish. Under the new Highways Act, every able - bodied man had to work, free of charge, on the roads for four full days each year. Churchmen and parishioners met yearly at Eastertide to choose two honest people to oversee and survey work on the highways of the Parish. They were unpaid and if they refused, they were fined £5. Doctors and clergymen were exempt but no one dared to suggest one of the gentry for the job. Every person with land worth £50 or more had to provide a cart drawn by oxen or horses and also two able - bodied men. Farmers had to contribute a man with a horse and every householder or labourer had to work as determined by the surveyor. Ten years later, in 1565, the work increased to six 8 - hour days' work. This was still not adequate to keep the roads in order; the increase of traffic, transporting goods, lime, stone, coal and cattle being moved by drovers, made the roads deteriorate rapidly.

From medieval times, southwest Wales was an important exporter of livestock. Many drovers attempted to avoid the bustle of driving large herds of cattle through towns, or along busy roads, and alternative routes were found. One such droving route ran from opposite the Commercial Inn at Llanddewi Velfrey through Llanfallteg to

Llanboidy. The Commercial Inn is now Commercial Cottage and was across the road from the Parc-y-Lan pub.

In 1771, an Act of Parliament obtained by around twelve of the local gentry of Narberth authorised a turnpike on the road from Commercial (now Llanddewi Velfrey) to Newcastle Emlyn. Initially, they were to be financed by loans at 4% interest, which were then paid for by tolls levied on road users at tollgates along the road network. The local tollgate was at Commercial.

The Rebecca Riots

By 1791, the newly formed Whitland Turnpike Trust became responsible for local roads. The income from tolls was not enough to improve the roads and toll prices rose. Farmers, who relied on transporting supplies, particularly lime and produce, found the toll roads very expensive. By 1839, local people were becoming increasingly agitated, not only with the cost of the toll road, but also with the enclosure of common land, bad harvests and an increase in tithes. They resented the privileged classes administering justice while the poor unemployed were forced into newly built workhouses. Then, when the Whitland Trust erected four new tollgates, local farmers decided enough was enough and they decided to act. Thus, the Rebecca Movement was formed in South Wales.

On the night of the 13th May 1839, just one week after it had been constructed, the Efailwen gate was destroyed and the tollhouse set on fire by a number of men disguised as women. The derivation of the '*daughters of Rebecca*' name is uncertain, but it may well be a biblical reference to Rebecca saying "*possess the gates of those which hate them*" (Genesis XXIV, 60). On the 6th June, a crowd of between 300 to 400 people, which must have included some from Llanfallteg, destroyed the gate at Efailwen for a second time. The protests continued for several years, peaking during 1843-44. Some of the instigators of the Rebecca Movement were eventually captured and a few were transported, but the reforms sought by the '*Daughters of Rebecca*' were eventually won and the number of tollgates on local roads was reduced.

Today we take our roads for granted, with little thought for the people who toiled on them.

THE CARDI BACH

The railway through Llanfallteg was well loved and known throughout the area as the '*Cardi Bach*'. Originally constructed to access the lead and silver mines at Llanfyrnach and the slate quarries at Glogue, it was not until 10th August 1885 that the railway was opened to Cardigan. An attempt by the Carmarthen and Cardigan Railway to build a broad gauge line failed in 1895 with the line only reaching as far as Newcastle Emlyn.

Plans for a Railway

John Owen, whose father was previously the proprietor of the Glogue Quarry, was the main instigator behind what was to become the Whitland and Tâf Vale Railway. He had approached James W. Szlumper from Aberystwyth, an engineer, in 1868 about building a standard gauge (4 foot 8.5 inch) railway from Whitland on the South Wales railway, later the Great Western Railway, to the quarries at Glogue and the Cardigan to Tenby road at Crymych.

James W Szlumper
©Crown copyright; RCAHMW.

It was generally accepted that railways were the answer to the problems of rural transport. The Government recognised conventional railways were so expensive that local communities could not afford to build them from their own resources. The Railway Construction Facilities Act of 1864 and the Regulation of Railways Act 1868 were introduced to provide for the construction of '*light railway*' rural lines.

The 1868 Act offered a solution to the transport problems of the Tâf Vale area. On the 1st July 1869 the Whitland and Tâf Vale Railway Company was incorporated with powers to construct and maintain a railway. Commencing from a junction on the South Wales Railway main line near Whitland and terminating at '*Crymmych Arms in Pembrokeshire County*'. It was built as a '*light railway*', and subject to the issue of the Board of Trade notice that no locomotive could exceed 16mph or be over 16 tons in weight.

348.—WHITLAND AND TAFF VALE.

Incorporated by 32 and 33 Vic., cap. 91 (12th July, 1869), to construct a railway from the South Wales section of the Great Western, near Whitland, to Crymmych-Arms, Pembrokeshire. Length, 16¼ miles. Capital, 37 000*l.* in 10*l.* shares and 12,500*l.* on loan. Great Western to provide a narrow gauge communication to Whitland, and to afford facilities.

The construction of the line was commenced in November last, and vigorous efforts are being made to open it for traffic in the course of the summer. The cost of the line, including land and preliminary expenses, will be about 2,600*l.* per mile.

No. of Directors—6; minimum, 3; quorum, 3 and 2. *Qualification, 200l.*

DIRECTORS:

Chairman—STEPHEN W. LEWIS, Esq., Regent Street, London.

David Davies, Esq., Llandinam, Montgomeryshire.	John Owen, Jun., Esq., Glogue Slate Quarries. Newcastle-Emlyn.
John Barrow, Esq., Ringwood, Chesterfield	William Owen, Esq., Withybush, Haverfordwest.
Benjamin Evans, Esq., Cyaigill, Cardigan.	

OFFICERS.—Sec., Howell Davies, Carmarthen; Eng., J. W. Szlumper, C.E., Aberystwyth; Solicitors, J. H. and R. Tyas and Huntington, London.

Offices—123, Lammas Street, Carmarthen.

Notice of Incorporation

The Whitland and Tâf Vale Act enabled the promoters to raise a capital of £37,000 in 3,700 £10 shares, with an additional £12,300 by loan upon the security of the Quarries at Glogue.

Five directors were appointed. The chairman was Stephen W. Lewis, landowner and businessman of Regent Street, London, and deputy chairman John Owen, quarry owner, Glogue, Pembrokeshire. The other directors were David Davies railway promoter, Llandinam,

Benjamin Evans of Cydigill, Cardigan, and Septimus S. Williamson, (shortly replaced by William Owen, brother of John Owen). In July 1869, Mr Howell Davies was appointed company secretary. The company offices were at 123 Lammas Street, Carmarthen.

The first formal meeting of the company took place on the 9th February 1869, at the Ivy Bush Royal Hotel, Carmarthen, when the Board approved the terms agreed by John Owen with Mr Szlumper.

The Parliamentary Bill for the railway was not unimpeded as there was a determined attempt to route the line through Llanboidy led by W.R.H. Powell of Maesgwynne, later to become M.P. for West Carmarthenshire. Yet a route to the north of Llanboidy continuing along the River Tigen to the Tâf Valley at Llanglydwen would have caused formidable constructional and operational problems.

The main railway line that ran along the boundary of Llanfallteg to the south was the broad gauge (7 foot) South Wales Railway, opened on 2nd January 1854, as a single track from Carmarthen to Haverfordwest. Later, on 1st July 1857, it was doubled and then eventually taken over by the G.W.R. in 1863.

Negotiations took place with G.W.R. to lay mixed gauge (7 foot and 4 foot 8.5 inch) track from Whitland station to the junction from which the Tâf Vale line would run. These stalled until 15th April 1869, when a meeting took place in the lobby of the House of Commons between the General Manager of the G.W.R. James Grierman and Stephen Lewis, John Owen, J. Szlumper, David Davies and Mr Bell (the Parliamentary Agent of the Whitland and Tâf Vale Railway), and terms and conditions were agreed that allowed the track laying to move forward.

In the autumn of 1869 the Whitland and Tâf Vale Railway issued a prospectus for the public to purchase its shares for a deposit of £1 per share. Describing the prospects of the new venture in glowing terms, the prospectus emphasised the valuable mineral and agricultural traffic, low construction costs and the very poor state of the roads.

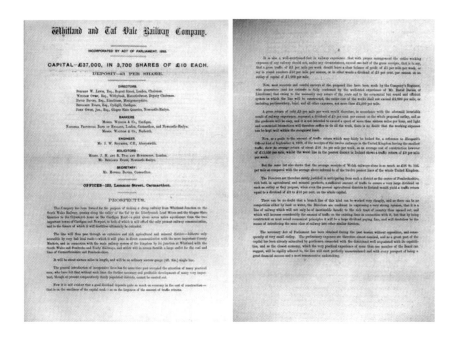

Share Prospectus

Negotiations with landowners did not go smoothly; at one stage John Owen exclaimed, *'one more vicar-landowner – would compel him to abandon the entire scheme!'* The most troublesome was Thomas Phillips (Twm Waunbwll) who would not allow surveyors on to his land. A court order was granted for access quickly followed, and the surveyors were chased by Thomas's notoriously untamed bulls, with Tom shouting at them to *'show the bulls your blue paper'*.

Building the railway

On 13th October 1870 the Board accepted the tender of Edward Lewis of £8,700 to construct the W. & T.V.R and on 8th November 1870 work commenced from the southern end.

In poor weather the track route was cleared of trees and undergrowth in half-mile sections and then ploughed. Gangs of ten men then laid a light railway along it to move materials from one section to another, as the roads were poor or non-existent.

It was reported at the Board meeting on 16th February 1871 that the contractor had completed five miles of earthworks and anticipated that mineral traffic to Llanglydwen Bridge would be possible by the early summer.

In April 1871, the Chairman, Stephen W. Lewis died and soon after the substantial shareholder and director, Mr J. Barrow, also died. A new acting Chairman, William Owen of Haverfordwest was appointed. Although the cost of construction was within estimates, insufficient capital had been subscribed and the Board faced financial difficulties.

By the end of June 1871 a temporary junction was installed with the Great Western Railway that gave access to Whitland Station. Track laying then commenced and on 4th January 1872 mineral trains first reached Llanglydwen.

The G.W.R. refused to allow W. & T.V.R. to keep its engines overnight at Whitland, so money was spent on the construction of an engine shed and workshop at Llanfallteg, which later became the headquarters of the Whitland and Cardigan Railway.

Llanfalteg locomotive shed

The G.W.R. took over the Whitland and Cardigan Railway on Tuesday, 31st August 1886, but the engine shed continued to be used until 1910.

The G.W.R. decided in May 1872 to convert all broad gauge (7 foot) rails to narrow gauge (4 foot 8.5 inch) and in Wales this was duly completed by 1st June 1872.

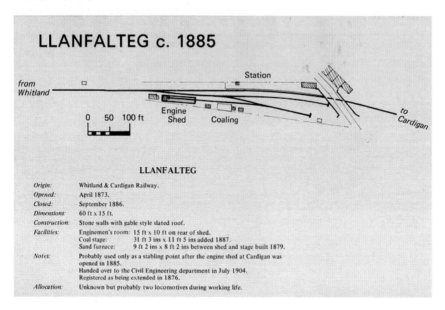

LLANFALTEG c. 1885

from Whitland

Station

to Cardigan

0   50   100 ft

Engine Shed   Coaling

LLANFALTEG

Origin:	Whitland & Cardigan Railway.
Opened:	April 1873.
Closed:	September 1886.
Dimensions:	60 ft x 15 ft.
Construction:	Stone walls with gable style slated roof.
Facilities:	Enginemen's room: 15 ft x 10 ft on rear of shed. Coal stage: 31 ft 3 ins x 11 ft 5 ins added 1887. Sand furnace: 9 ft 2 ins x 8 ft 2 ins between shed and stage built 1879.
Notes:	Probably used only as a stabling point after the engine shed at Cardigan was opened in 1885. Handed over to the Civil Engineering department in July 1904. Registered as being extended in 1876.
Allocation:	Unknown but probably two locomotives during working life.

By August 1872 the line was ballasted from the Great Western Railway main line, now called Tâf Vale Junction to Llanglydwen. On completion of ballasting to Glogue, the permanent way was ready for traffic. When the Board met on 21st October 1872 it was suggested the line could be open for heavy goods traffic early in November. They agreed to obtain a locomotive, wagons and a brake van. Evan Pugh as an engine driver was appointed on a wage of 6s. 0d. a day. Thomas Davies became a fireman on 3s. 6d. a day and Evan Thomas became the engineer cleaner on a wage of 2s. 8d. a day. On 1st March 1873, John Davis was appointed to guard and later as stationmaster at Llanfyrnach, with Benjamin Davies taking over as a guard on 4s. 0d. a day.

A 0-6-0 saddle tank locomotive engine was bought for £1,600. Built by Messrs. Fox Walker and Co., of Atlas Works Bristol the locomotive (Works No 170) was considered *'perfect in every respect'*. It was named *'John Owen'* as a tribute to the pioneer of the railway who became its Chairman on 1st March 1872.

**Whitland and Tâf Valley loco no 1,
renumbered under GWR to 1385**

Line opening

Colonel Hutchinson, the Government Inspector, examined the Tâf Vale Junction on 15th March and after a few slight additions a Board of Trade certificate was issued and the railway was officially opened for goods and minerals on Monday 24th March 1873 between Whitland and the slate quarries at Glogue. The initial freight service consisted of two trains a day in both directions over the whole route. The line was extended to Crymych by early July 1874. Consent to carry passengers came later after heavy investment in signals and associated equipment at Llanfallteg, as well as the Blaenavon and Penclippin level crossings, Login, Llanglydwen, Rhydowen and Llanfyrnach stations, Glogue sidings and Crymych station.

There were level crossings at both Llanfallteg and Llanfyrnach stations. There were a further seven public level crossings and 49 underline bridges or culverts throughout the length of the railway. Station buildings were small wooden sheds standing on low platforms. Train staff controlled the crossings by working absolute block telegraphic systems throughout from Tâf Vale Junction to its terminus at Crymmych Arms, a distance of 14 miles 29 chains. The steepest gradients had an incline of 1 in 35.

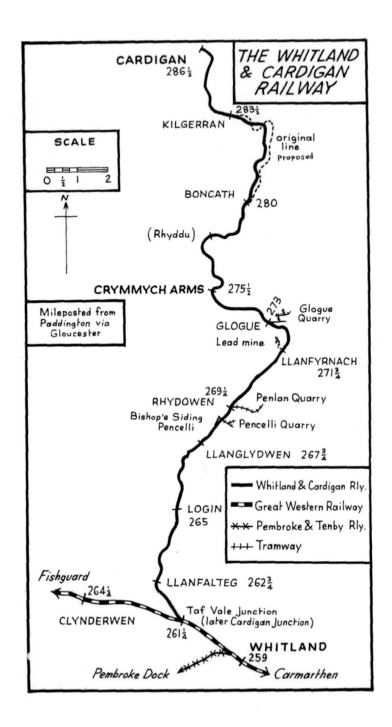

THE WHITLAND
& CARDIGAN
RAILWAY

CARDIGAN
286½

283½

KILGERRAN

original
line
Proposed

BONCATH
280

(Rhyddu)

SCALE

0 ½ 1 2

N

CRYMMYCH ARMS ← 275½

273¼

Mileposted from
Paddington via
Gloucester

GLOGUE
Lead mine

Glogue
Quarry

LLANFYRNACH
271¾

269½

RHYDOWEN

Penlan Quarry

Bishop's Siding
Pencelli

Pencelli Quarry

LLANGLYDWEN 267¾

━━━ Whitland & Cardigan Rly.

▨▨▨ Great Western Railway

✕✕ Pembroke & Tenby Rly.

╬╬╬ Tramway

LOGIN
265

Fishguard

264½

LLANFALTEG 262¾

CLYNDERWEN

261¼

Taf Vale Junction
(later Cardigan Junction)

WHITLAND
259

Pembroke Dock

Carmarthen

70

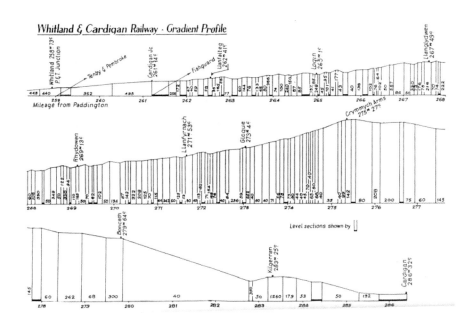

Gradient profile of line

The route was subject to a strict speed limit of 16 mph throughout at this time. This was only increased to 30 mph after G.W.R. upgraded the track from Cardigan Junction to Crymmych Arms.

All services were provided by the Whitland and Tâf Vale Company using its own locomotive and rolling stock. The company also acquired twelve goods vehicles from the British Wagon Co., ten open wagons, one goods van and one 'brak*e*' van and work continued in preparation for the introduction of passenger services. Six 4-wheeled passenger vehicles were ordered from the Gloucester Wagon Company, these being 21 ft 2ins long and constructed of teak. Documents show that there were two First/Second Luggage, two Brake Thirds and two Third Luggage vehicles.

Start of Passenger Services

In the summer of 1875 James Szlumper declared that the railway was ready for its public opening between Whitland and Crymmych Arms and notice was given to the Board of Trade for the final inspection on 29th June 1875. Colonel Rich R.E. was appointed to carry it out, but he did not do so within the allotted ten days by statute. The Whitland

and Tâf Vale Railway minutes record: *'The chairman and engineer waited for him especially at Carmarthen Station for three days and on 10th July no communication whatever having been received from Colonel Rich, it was determined that on 12th July 1875, a passenger service was inaugurated over the new railway.'*

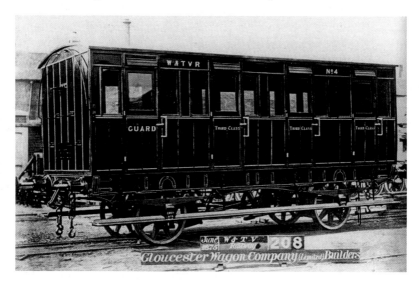

One of the new Brake Thirds

The railway had been opened for the carriage of passengers without a formal Board of Trade inspection and Colonel Rich R.E. of the Board of Trade carried this out retrospectively a few days later.   The Colonel was reasonably satisfied with the new line but in his report of 17th July 1875 he stipulated a number of improvements, including second platforms at the passing stations, better lineside fencing and the provision of station clocks, the construction of '*lodges*' at each of the public level crossings, adjustments to crossing gates and to some points and signals.

The original passenger train service consisted of four workings in each direction with an average journey time for the 16.5 mile trip between Whitland and Crymmych Arms of 80 minutes. The passenger trains between Whitland and Crymych were timed to connect with G.W.R. trains at Whitland but the day would start with a train from Llanfallteg to Whitland.

The first locomotive No 1 – '*John Owen*' was unable to work the service on its own and a second locomotive of generally similar design was brought from Messrs Fox and Walker and Co. in 1875. No 2 was another 0-6-0- ST with 3 foot 6 inch wheels. A third 0-6-0-ST was supplied by them in 1877 with inside cylinders and 4 foot wheels. All three locomotives were based in the engine shed at Llanfallteg, which had rudimentary maintenance facilities.

Llanfallteg crossing in 1912

The introduction of passenger services did much to rescue the dire financial position of the company and at the half - yearly ordinary general meeting held at the Yelverton Arms Hotel in Whitland on the 29th February 1876, a report from the Board affirmed… that since the opening for passengers ... '*the traffic has exceeded the expectations of your Directors. Up to 31st December 1875 the railway had carried 446 first class, 949 second class and 17,085 third class passengers producing receipts of £848. 15s. 10d. Merchandise and minerals produced £1381. 0s. 4d. and mails £163. 13s. 8d. After meeting all charges against revenue a balance of £1,020. 12s. 4d. remained ... the recommended dividend was accepted and this took up £555 of the balance.*'

In addition to the normal services, a number of excursions were run from Crymmych Arms to Whitland in connection with special G.W.R. services. These sometimes utilised normal branch services. At other times a '*special*' was run. Most of these were advertised at '*cheap excursion*' rates (e.g. in October 1881 Crymych to Whitland - ls. 6d.,

Llanfallteg 5d. return fares).   Eisteddfods featured regularly in these *specials* including those at Whitland, Clynderwen and Narberth. The visit of the Prince of Wales to Swansea on Tuesday 18th October 1881 generated yet another connecting train to Whitland. The Tivy Side Hunt's steeplechase and hurdle races in 1883 generated a connecting morning special from Whitland to Crymych, returning in the evening to connect with G.W.R. trains serving stations to Pembroke Dock and Neath.

Passenger Services 1910–1958

Bradshaw's timetable April 1910

Bradshaw's timetable July 1922

Bradshaw's timetable July 1938

Bradshaw's timetable September 1958

Timetables of Passenger Services 1910-1958

The safety record of the *'Cardi Bach'* was generally good, although there were a number of mishaps in the early years caused in the main by engine failures and derailments. In Llanfyrnach on 22nd June 1877, there was a fatal accident when a woman attempting to cross the line in front of the up mail train was killed. A second fatality occurred near Llanglydwen in 1923 and another near Llanfallteg when the victims were walking on the line. In each of the cases the train driver was exonerated. A tragic accident near Llanfallteg on the 25th August 1885 causing three fatalities was linked to the fact that it occurred on the evening of Crymych Fair.

Extension to Cardigan

The first steps towards extending the line to Cardigan were taken in 1876. Encouraged by wide support and Parliamentary backing was sought for its construction and a bill was prepared in 1877. It passed quickly without opposition through both Houses of Parliament. The commencement of work was delayed until August 1878; progress being frustrated by difficulties relating to the acquisition of land. A Mr D.G. Davies of Cardigan was particularly obstructive and had to be bought off with £1000 in fully paid shares. The purchase of the rails was completed however, at the *'unprecedented low price of £3.12s. 6d. per ton'* and with the whole consignment of 1200 tons being stacked at Crymych and Cardigan.

Financial crises were always close at hand, and worsened when James Szlumper resigned under acrimonious circumstances and obtained substantial compensation. David Davies at this time was demanding repayment of £14,000 of debentures and the G.W.R. lost no time in taking advantage of the situation in forcing payment of a trading debt of £3,800. The situation was so bad that the rails purchased at low cost were seized by court bailiffs to satisfy a judgement. The directors had to borrow money personally to recover them. Eventually it was agreed in August 1881 that the G.W.R. would help the Whitland and Cardigan Railway to complete its 11 mile extension.

In September 1881, shortly after the passing of the Whitland and Cardigan Railway Act, the G.W.R. Chairman, Sir Daniel Gooch, visited the West Wales area to see the Tâf Vale Railway. He took a journey over the branch from Crymmych Arms in company with John Owen. Sir Daniel was not particularly impressed by the condition of the line and on 10th September 1881 he recorded the following note in his diary: *'After lunch we left Mr Gower and he sent his carriage with us to the Crymmych Arms (sic) station where we took the three p.m. train to our Whitland station. Mr Owen the chairman of this branch accompanied me over his line. It is not in a very good state. I suppose we will one day take it over. At Whitland I had a special which ran us down to Neyland in time for dinner. The day has been fine'.*

Construction of the Cardigan extension began in May 1883, the engineer being John B. Walton, and the contractors Messrs. Appleby and Lawton. By August 1885 the permanent way was completed as far as Cardigan and on 10th August the Whitland and Cardigan directors organised an excursion train leaving Cardigan at 7.00 a.m. for Tenby with *'through carriages'* returning from the coast at 6.00 p.m. The line was still far from complete so the extension could not be opened for regular public services. The company was desperately short of money; a dispute arose over additional works on the extension line as the original line was also in need of substantial upgrading. The crisis deepened with the death of the Chairman, John Owen, early in June 1886 at the age of 68 years.

A G.W.R. take-over of the struggling local railway moved rapidly towards a conclusion but under the terms of the earlier agreement this could not take place until the Cardigan extension had been opened for passenger traffic. The line had to be *'passed'* by the Board of Trade, and the necessary Board of Trade inspection was arranged for 29th and 30th June again by Colonel F.H.R. Rich. On this occasion the inspecting officer found much to criticise. The station buildings had not been completed, a 3000-gallon water tank had not been delivered and works on the signals were unfinished. As a result the opening was postponed for one month from 6th July.

A further problem arose in connection with the original line. The company had still not provided the sleeping accommodation for the crossing gatekeepers that Colonel Rich had required following his earlier inspection in 1875. Accordingly, steps were taken to attend to the lodges at Penclippin and Rhydowen at once. At Llanglydwen and

Llanfyrnach rooms were to be built over the stations and at Llanfallteg and Glogue it was agreed that lodges were not needed because local cottages could be rented. It was subsequently agreed that the G.W.R. would construct the necessary sleeping accommodation within a specified time and so the Board of Trade Inspector allowed the line to be opened to Cardigan for the carriage of passengers. The first trains ran on Tuesday 31st August 1886, and having demonstrated their railway was complete, the Whitland and Cardigan directors were able to hand over the branch line to the G.W.R. under the terms of the operating agreement.

Regular G.W.R. services commenced on the following day, Wednesday 1st September 1886. The first train to arrive carried officials and 100 children given a free ride from Crymych, and was welcomed by the Mayor, a brass band and a 'hundred tradesmen.'

Some 55 years later, a group of what might be called 'very important persons' travelled the full length of the 'Cardi Bach' railway and back. On Friday 11th April 1941, the Prime Minister, Winston Churchill, Mrs Churchill and their daughter Mary, John Winant (the U.S.A. Ambassador), Lord Ismay and others went by train to Cardigan and then by car to Aberporth where they saw a 'noisy but interesting display of rockets and U.P. projectiles'. They slept on the train that night 'at a wayside station called Whitland' before travelling to Bristol on the following day. (U.P. projectiles were 'Unrotated Projectiles', a type of anti-aircraft missile.)

On Thursday 28th November 1957, the Royal Train, with His Royal Highness the Duke of Edinburgh aboard, travelled up towards Cardigan, stopping overnight at Glogue. The next day the Duke opened a new extension to the Cardigan County School before visiting the Royal Aircraft Establishment at Aberporth the following day.

For the Tâf Valley, Cardigan and north-east Pembrokeshire the new railway rapidly became its economic lifeline. The Glogue Quarry and Llanfyrnach lead mine were the immediate benefactors, but in the late 1870s quarry materials were also transported from Pengelli quarry near Llanglydwen and Penlan Quarry at Rhydowen by tramways to the railway line. These proved unsuccessful and were soon abandoned. Slates produced in Tyrdi Quarry near Llangolman were railed from Llanglydwen until 1957. However, the Glogue Quarry did not prosper as expected and closed down in 1926. The Llanfyrnach lead mines closed in 1890, the last year's output being a mere 10 tons.

Other than quarry materials, agricultural produce provided the bulk of the outward traffic. Large numbers of livestock were loaded at Crymych and Cardigan and were a large source of revenue for the railway until the 1950s. The railway stations became collecting points for farm milk with the establishment of Whitland and Cardigan milk factories. These were superseded by farm gate collections by road transport by 1950. Before farm marketing of bulk liquid milk, butter from local markets would be processed and transported by rail to industrial towns in South Wales. Butter continued to be carried, but it was now mainly New Zealand butter, brought in and blended and packed in Llanglydwen. In the depression years of the early 1930s rabbits were also exported in large quantities throughout South Wales and the Midlands, only ceasing in the mid 1950s with the outbreak of myxomatosis.

Stations became the growth points of rural businesses, and all the needs of the community not locally produced came in by rail. Animal feed, fertilisers, coal, timber, building materials and household goods were all delivered to the local stations until in the early 1950s, when a widespread switch to road transport followed the growth of road haulage companies.

The social impact of the railway, especially the first section from Whitland to Crymych, was immense. It brought new communities to life. There was no direct line of communication along the valley of the Tâf before the arrival of the railway. The road journey from Whitland to Llanfallteg is five miles on the western side through Llanddewi Velfrey and nearly six miles on the eastern side of the valley. The railway journey was 3.25 miles. Llanfallteg to Login by road is six miles one way and five miles another compared with 2.25 miles by rail. The pattern is the same between Login and Llanglydwen, from Llanglydwen and Rhydowen and onwards to Crymych.

The 'Cardi Bach' created a rural community of closely-knit villages where none existed before. It had widely applicable consequences for the hamlet of Rhyd-ddol-esgob which lay to the south of the river Tâf, as the engine shed and Llanfallteg station were sited there. A few cottages were demolished and new terraced houses constructed to provide homes for local railway workers. With the opening of the railway line engine drivers, footplate firemen, guards, stationmasters, porters, clerks, cleaners, repair gangs and crossing keepers were needed. The workers were paid in cash with wages more regular and higher than most of them were accustomed to in agriculture.

Early Llanfallteg Railway Workers

THOMAS EVANS was a railway ganger or platelayer who lived at Bridgend, Llanfallteg, and was possibly one of the first railway workers to live in the village.

JAMES BEYNON was a railway platelayer and later a railway ganger. He was born in Llanddewi Velfrey c.1845, lived at Waundelyn, Llanfallteg initially, but later moved in1885 to Dandderwen.

GRIFFITH JOHN, born c.1842, was a railway signalman. He lived at Bridgend, Llanfallteg, with his spouse Ruth and two children.

HENRY EVANS, born c.1856, was a railway engine cleaner. He lived near the station, at the Railway Inn, Llanfallteg.

BENJAMIN and HANNAH DAVIES were railway guards, Benjamin from Llanfallteg, born c.1850, Hannah from Castell Dwyran, born in 1849.

WILLIAM LLOYD, a railway packer and platelayer, was born in St. Dogmaels, Pembrokeshire and lived in 3 Adams Street, then 3 Adams Row, for over twenty years.

DAVID ROBERTS was a railway inspector and lived at No.2 Glenview, Llanfallteg. David had come to Llanfallteg from Montgomeryshire.

JOSEPH SALMON of Dolgwernen, Llanfallteg was a railway engine driver.

THOMAS MATHIAS, born c.1829, was a labourer on the railway, living at Dolwen-isaf, Llanfallteg,

DAVID DAVIES was a stoker and lived at the Railway Station Llanfallteg.

THOMAS PHILLIPS was the stationmaster at the Railway Station, Llanfallteg, for over twenty years and lived at Rhydywrach, Llanfallteg. Martha Phillips, his youngest daughter, was a telegraph clerk in the early 1900s possibly working at the railway station with her father.

LEWIS GAWES was a railway ganger or platelayer and lived at No.1 Dandderwen, Llanfallteg.

EDWARD GRIFFITHS was a railway plate packer and lived at College, Llanfallteg.

DAVID MORGAN was a railway plate packer; born in the 1880s who lived at Penbontbren, and later Compton House.

GEORGE JOHN was a railway engine driver, living at the local lodging house, No.1 Glenview, Llanfallteg.

HENRY THOMAS lodged at No.1 Glenview. He worked at the nearby railway station and was employed as an engine cleaner.

CALEB EDWARDS, a railway platelayer, was born c.1842 and lived at Troedyrhyw, Llanfallteg.

THOMAS ROWLANDS, a railway platelayer during the 1880s, came to the area from Carno, Montgomeryshire and lived at Dolwen-isaf, Llanfallteg, then moved to Penybont Farm, Llanfallteg.

LEWIS JAMES, a railway ganger, lived at No.2 Dandderwen, Llanfallteg.

DAVID THOMAS was a railway platelayer born in Llangan c. 1865 and lived at Fron, Llanfallteg.

WILLIAM EDWARDS was a platelayer on the railway and lived at Glenview, Llanfallteg.

JANE PERKINS, originally from Llanboidy, was the railway-crossing keeper at Penclippin Crossing.

THOMAS OWEN was a railway platelayer and lived at Hiraeth, Llanfallteg.

Closure

In the years immediately after the Second World War the extension of car ownership seriously reduced passenger use of the *'Cardi Bach'*. Following the easing of fuel rationing and wartime restrictions, road transport expanded rapidly in the 1950s and the loss of freight traffic dealt another blow to the commercial viability of the line. In February 1962, British Railways obtained the approval of the Transport Users Consultative Committee to withdraw passenger services; this took effect on the following 8th September at the end of the summer timetable.

Typical train in Llanfallteg station in 1959

After some weeks carrying more passengers than usual, the final day of the railway saw more passengers than any one could remember. Amongst them was Herbert James, aged over 80, who could recall his *'marvellous trip'* on the first journey to Cardigan on 1st September 1886. He was the only person to travel on the first and last train. When the last train pulled out of Whitland it carried about 50 passengers in three coaches. By the time it reached Cardigan it had about 500 crammed on board.

Last Train 1963

The last train in 1963
(Mr and Mrs Morgan – Siop)

After many whistles, cheers and laments the train returned slowly to
Whitland, passing sightseers at all the stations on the line. The
locomotive, appropriately, was '4569' which had been a familiar sight

of the railway for many years. The driver was Gilbert Lye, the fireman O. Glover and the passenger guard Mr Williams.

The freight service continued until May 1963.

Sources

Copsey, John (Ed). Research Stanley Jenkins & Chris Turner. *Great Western Railway Journal No 30 Spring 1999*

Davies, D Hywel. *Carmarthenshire Antiquary* Vol XXXIV D , 1998

Hale, Michael. *Steam in South Wales Vol 2 North and West of Swansea/* Oxford Publishing Co, 1981.

Price, M.R.C. *The Whitland and Cardigan Railway* Oakwood Press 1976 1st Edition, 1991 2nd Edition.

RECENT TIMES: 19th & 20th Centuries

Land ownership

Until the coming of the railway in the 1870s nearly all of the inhabitants of the parish were involved in agriculture. Most of the cottages had land attached to them and were rented. By 1914 less than 12% of all holdings nationally of more than one acre were owner occupied. Wages were low, typically a shilling a day for a farm worker, and if food was provided 4d would be deducted: disposable income was non-existent.

Two of the largest landowners in the region, the Morgans of Tegfynydd, and the Gowers of Pengwern, Clynderwen House and Castell Malgwyn, were increasing the size of their estates despite income from their lands reducing yearly. Their estate expansions were funded by shrewd and successful investments associated with the huge industrial growth in manufacturing and transportation, or by raising mortgages. They modified their estate structure to optimise farm size, enabling their tenants to make a reasonable living and also increasing the rentable value.

From 1850 farm prices fell considerably due to free trade agreements. Cheap grain came in from the USA, Canada and Australia, soon to be followed by meat in the new refrigerated holds of fast ships. Farm incomes suffered throughout the UK; farmers strove to cut costs and reduced labour-intensive corn production. In addition to their permanent staff, large farms needed the labour from about six small farms; reducing their labour requirement forced men to leave this area to find work to support their families. They often sought work in industrial towns or the mines. A report on the 1851 census mentioned the shortage of men in Llanfallteg and Hiraeth due to the number leaving to work in the mines in Glamorganshire.

Agricultural employment

Employment for the majority would have been irregular, on a casual basis, and would be weather dependent. The jobs would be manual and farm labouring: typically hay making, cereal harvesting in the summer, and fencing, faggoting and ditching in the winter. Pay was not necessarily cash; labour debts were incurred and repaid by labour or food. The 1850s was not a cash economy - money changed hands infrequently and an informal credit and debit system prevailed.

An agreement between a tenant of an eight acre holding and his landlord in 1851 stated: *'Agreed with tenant for £5 5s 0d per year, and he is to work for 6d per day all round the year. 2 meals of meat from Michaelmas to St David's day and from then 3 meals to Michaelmas. He is bound to work with me whenever I will and not go anywhere else without my consent and he is to pay the above rent taxes and tithes belonging to the above mentioned farm, he is now in possession of -----'*

The tenant would have to work for 35 weeks just to pay the rent, leaving little time left to work on his own farm: so his wife and family probably tended their stock and did other chores such as milking the cow and making butter.

Houses

In Victorian times many houses were rebuilt of stone with roofs made of slate from the quarry at Glogue. However, most labourers may still have lived in old cottages. In a letter to the Royal Commission in 1867 the Rev. William Owen reported that in south Wales *'the state of the labourers' cottages is very bad; badly constructed; one floor and one room on that floor, partly divided by some article of furniture; damp walls; earth floors; smoky chimnies; a small window or two, often no more than a square foot, and never opened; no out-offices, or any accommodation whatever'.*

The Commission also reported that *'The ordinary form of a cottage in South Wales is a rectangular building about 20 feet by 12 (inside measurement) with walls of mud (clay and straw mixed) or stone about 8 feet high. The mud cottage is almost always covered with straw thatch. In the middle of the front wall is the door with a small window on each side. Running back from each side of the door for 6 or 8 feet, and almost as high as the door are partitions, often formed by the back of a box bed or chest of drawers, by means of which partitions the inside space is divided into two small rooms, in one of which is a wide fireplace surmounted by a conical chimney. The whole interior is open to the roof, except where boards or wattled hurdles are stuck across the heads of the walls to support children's beds. The floor is usually of mud or puddled clay. The only outside office is the pigsty, generally built against the end of the cottage. Such is a description of probably four-fifths of the labourers' cottages in the districts I visited.'*

Judging by the state of the cottages, it may have been an attractive option to *'go into service'* and work as live-in servants in farmhouses and the more affluent households.

Farm Practice

In south west Wales before 1900 a farmer's cash income came mainly from the sale of store cattle, pigs, horses, or heavily salted butter in 20 to 30 lbs tubs or 100 to 120 lbs casks.

During the 1880s wheat production surpassed barley production, and replaced barley for bread making. Barley was used to make beer and feed the cattle and pigs; oats for oat cakes, porridge and horse feed. Hay was made for winter feed for all the stock. Vegetables, roots and potatoes were grown for home consumption, and to feed pigs and cattle.

Wooden plough in use from Medieval times until the 19th century. First drawn by oxen then later by heavy horses.

In 1900 around 30 acres was considered to be the smallest unit that constituted a farm capable of supporting a farmer and his family. The farm generally had its own equipment and a pair of horses usually known as a one pair place (*lle par o geffyle*). Smaller holdings had to have additional income perhaps acting as hauliers, or maybe dealing in butter and eggs, or slaughtering pigs.

A typical 20 - acre holding kept six cows, two acres of corn, ten rows of potatoes and four rows of mangolds. A neighbouring farm might send two men and a pair of horses to till the two acres in a day. A cart was sent to move and spread the manure to the potato patch and also at haymaking. No cash payment was made but a labour debt was incurred and probably paid back at harvest time when all hands were needed.

Smaller holdings under 15 acres would probably not have horses but kept cows to provide milk, butter and cheese and a calf to sell. They were known as a cow place (*lle buwch*). Oats and potatoes were grown to feed the family and the cow. The oats might be kept on a larger farm where it could be threshed, with the smallholder providing casual labour to the larger farms.

The occupants of cottages without land were called cottagers and frequently an arrangement was made with a farmer to grow potatoes to feed the family and fatten a pig, incurring a labour debt to be repaid at harvest. Many cottagers might be growing potatoes on the same farm, thus incurring another labour debt.

Farms of 100 acres, a considerable place (*lle jogel*), would perhaps have 20 acres of corn, which a servant working a pair of horses would prepare for sowing, starting in January and traditionally finishing by the last week in April, just before Barley Saturday at Cardigan. This is still held in April with the traditional show and parade of stallions. It would take the servant a full four month's work due to weather conditions and often required a second servant and pair of horses, hence the expression '*two pair place*'.

Ploughing was the work of a servant (*gwas*) who worked the horses. He was generally unmarried and lived over the stable, as he had to look after the horses from early morning to late at night. After marriage he would become a labourer and cease working with horses, have a different contract and be found some other accommodation. The farm labourer (*gweithwr*) probably spent the winter hedging and ditching. The first servant was called '*gwas mawr*', and the second servant, whether a maid, a boy or petty servant was a '*crwe gwas bach'*. Agricultural labourers were traditionally hired at Michaelmas (29th September) for a year.

When the corn had been harvested the servant usually threshed it. The barn handmaid's first job was to collect up the straw

Reaper- binder introduced in the late 19th century and in use until the advent of the combine harvester.

after threshing by the flail. When threshing machines replaced flailing the second part of her job remained if flour was to be made - that of drying the grain, tending the fire and turning the grains on the rack in the kiln.

A 200-acre farm would need 40 acres of corn and at harvest time required approximately 100 working labour days. Large farms needed a large labour force at haymaking and harvest time, supplemented by the cottagers and other small neighbouring farms: often the whole family was involved. As well as being fed with meat, the farmer's wife often gave buttermilk and oatmeal to the workers. Frequently, a number of farms would co-operate at busy times sharing labour, horses and equipment, as everything depended on bringing in the crops while the weather held.

Most holdings kept a cow but only the larger holdings had a bull. Cows had to be taken to the bull, incurring yet another labour debt. It was customary to give a penny as '*luck money*' to the maid that released the bull into the yard with the visiting cow.

The railways

The Carmarthen to Haverfordwest railway completed in 1845 ran through the Gower estate about 150 metres south of St. Mallteg's Church. Some farm restructuring was necessary; Penpwll Isaf was sited right next to the line and was abandoned. The line also passed through the middle of the clay pits for the brickyard.

The railway construction workers (navvies) worked in gangs of 20 to 100 and would have needed somewhere to quench their thirst, particularly on payday. They would have bought eggs, milk, butter, cheese and fresh bread locally, stimulating the local economy enormously for a very short period of time. Cash would have changed hands, as navvies were '*here today and gone tomorrow*'.

Life was pretty tough for those looking to agriculture for an income in 1870 when a decision was made to build a railway from Whitland to Cardigan. This had far reaching consequences for the hamlet of Rhyd-ddol-esgob, centred on the east side of the river, as Llanfallteg station and engine sheds were sited here. Some cottages were demolished and terraced houses built to provide accommodation for the railway workers and one of the Plas-y-pwdel cottages became the Railway Inn.

The new railway lines created a huge demand for labour. Many farm workers left, opting instead for industrial or commercial employment and higher wages. Once built, engine drivers, firemen, crossing keepers, a stationmaster, porters, cleaners and repair gangs were all needed. Permanent railway employees were paid in cash, with wages higher than they had known in agriculture. The village grew considerably and clearly prospered with a cash based economy. Farmers, merchants, blacksmiths and other trade people all had increased demand for their produce and wares and business expanded. Not everyone was happy, some farms and holdings were cut in half by the railway line, although there was compensation: Mary Thomas of Penclippen received £250, '*understood to be £50 for the land and £200 for the severance and other damage*'.

Almost everybody worked where they lived. Although the railway had recently arrived, commuting to work was not yet a realistic option. Fares were relatively high and only railway workers were allowed to travel free to their place of work. Agriculture was still the main employment: there were 25 farmers and a further 34 people worked directly in agriculture (a third of the working population in the village). Nowadays, less than a handful make their primary living from farming. A quarter of the working population worked as servants, nearly all of them living in their place of work. Many worked in farmhouses, but apart from Tegfynydd mansion and the clergy very few people could afford servants. Interestingly, three railway employees, the engine driver, guard and inspector had servants.

End of cottage industries

In 1881 twenty-nine people in Llanfallteg worked making clothing and footwear. There were five male tailors and ten female dressmakers, plus four seamstresses. Additionally, there was a milliner and a stocking knitter. Nine men made shoes, six classifying themselves as shoemakers, and three as clog makers.

Thanks to the railway, those who had set up cottage industries such as clog making and tailoring, were now faced with products from the industrial heartlands arriving in the village very quickly and cheaply by rail, undercutting their hand-made products by anything from 25% to 40%.

Half of the women worked at home, doing laborious chores without modern labour saving gadgets. Employment opportunities for women were particularly limited: 60% of the remainder worked in domestic service (predominantly the younger women), whilst the remainder worked in dressmaking or as agricultural workers.

In 1881 very few people could afford the luxury of retiring. There were only eight annuitants in the village. The remainder had to continue working as long as they could, relying on relatives if they became too infirm to work. Nor was life much easier for children: the oldest scholars were 14; one ten year old boy was working as a labourer and several 12 and 13 year old girls were working as domestic servants.

Although the village prospered, the parish farms as a whole were in a pretty poor state. Some tenancies changed hands regularly and some tenants left to find an easier living. Others moved to large or small-holdings as landlords manipulated rents to attract 'proven' farm tenants, thus securing a small but regular income for themselves.

Casual farm workers who could find work on the railway had better working conditions with a higher and regular income. In 1891 Edward Griffiths lived on a 5-acre holding, College Cottage on the

Tegfynydd Estate. He was a skilled worker, a railway plate packer, and in 1920 he and his wife Mary, with their son George, managed to purchase their tenanted holding of 30 acres for £500 when it was sold at auction.

The Great War

The next major event of influence was the start of the First World War. 1915 saw a huge requirement for horses, food and wood: prices rose with demand. Farming was booming again and land prices increased. In 1916 the start of the U boat war caused the government to introduce measures to increase food production, particularly grain. Farm mechanisation advanced with thrashing machines, reapers, binders and mowing machines beginning to appear in West Wales, although tractors were still rare. Draught horses were in great demand both by farmers, and by the military, who could compulsorily purchase them. Due to the shortage of labour, with the military recruiting young men, women were encouraged to seek farm work.

The village experienced full employment and farm prices were high, whilst taxation increased. The landed gentry provided many of the young officers for the British army, and fatalities of commissioned officers were disproportionately higher than men from the ranks. Death duties, which were first introduced in 1894, and increased taxation, started to have a profound effect. This led to a nationwide redistribution of wealth.

Between the Wars

In 1919, with the war over, demand from the military reduced. Some of those that saw military service did not return to agriculture, as industry had more employment opportunities and better pay. Food imports from the New World restarted so farm prices had to fall and rents were reduced. Britain was undergoing large social and economic changes. The war created a large national debt, vastly increased taxation and death duties, coupled with low incomes. This precipitated changes in land ownership - often enforced. The landed gentry sold off land, often by auction, so giving the sitting tenant an opportunity to buy. By this time the Gowers and Morgans no longer owned land in the village. Historically land had been inherited by a few individuals or purchased by industrial wealth. Land prices were low, so many people, mostly tenant farmers, had an opportunity to buy land. Sitting tenants had a further discount.

The village and surrounding area lost more of its small cottage industries. They could not compete with the factory - made products. By the early 1920s clog makers, shirt makers and tailors were disappearing and the brickworks closed in 1935. The corn mill also closed in about 1940.

The stock market crash of 1929 put further pressure on to the estate owning gentry, industrialists and small businesses alike. Many were shut down or abandoned. Farm values fell even further as more land was put up for sale. Farmers and smallholders could still make a living despite reduced farm gate prices, provided that only the bare minimum of farm labour was hired. Horses still outnumbered tractors; fewer acres of corn were grown, and then usually for home consumption as cattle and horse feed.

There were many opportunities to rent houses, smallholdings or farms in the area in the early 1930s despite the knowledge that the return was small and the hours long. Even so, many people were prepared to have a go at farming. With the country in recession and millions unemployed or on strike against lower wages, prospective tenants had very little to lose.

Farm to farm co-operation still thrived, but the farm cottager dependency had all but disappeared. The mines and quarries at Llanfyrnach and Glogue were in decline, leaving less for the railway to transport. In 1933, however, the Milk Marketing Board was formed, with a guaranteed market for milk. This was an impetus for many farmers to start or expand milk production and cowsheds and dairies were built on smallholdings as well as on the larger farms. Milk travelled by rail to the milk factory in Whitland, which was operated by United Dairies. It was a new opportunity for many who had reasonable access to the railway station. Income was guaranteed - payment was prompt and the margin over costs was small but adequate. A lifeline had been thrown to local farmers and smallholders, and it was taken with both hands. Most of the milking was done by hand and often children were encouraged to help Mum and Dad. Small herds consisted of only 5 or 6 cows, 14 to 18 was a good number for a 30 to 40 - acre holding. Carmarthenshire soon had the largest number of milk producers relative to area in the United Kingdom.

World War II

Once again, in 1939, with the outbreak of war the U boats endangered food imports. The British Government created a Ministry of Food, formed local county-based committees to direct farm operations, with the power to evict an owner-occupier. Schemes were created to encourage farm expansion and efficiency and included land drainage, hedge removal, liming and reseeding and there was an edict that all farms must sow and harvest 10% of their holding in cereals as directed by the committee. Many thousands of acres of permanent pasture were ploughed; the government also provided tractors, ploughs and tractor drivers where it was necessary. All food production increased but only with the essential help of many hundreds of thousands of women from the Women's Land Army - volunteers at first and later by government direction. Agriculture was booming again in a wartime economy.

The 10% cereal rule caused much animosity among the farming community. Some said that much of the extreme west of the U.K. was not suitable for cereals and should be kept in grass for greater efficiency. Lack of experience in crop husbandry, together with fuel shortages, and ploughing tractors failing to arrive at the appropriate time of the year contributed to some dismal crop yields. Yet the 10% rule persisted. Every last acre of even the smallest holding came under scrutiny from the committee. Woods and trees were cut down with or without the owner's permission as timber imports all but stopped.

During the war, troops were stationed all over the country. Tegfynydd Mansion and Clynderwen House were commandeered by the military and there was a U.S. Army barracks at Penpwll, near the railway line where some sidings were built.

At the end of the war, in 1945, food was in short supply. The Women's Land Army was not disbanded until late 1947 and some prisoners of war could elect to stay and work on the farms. Mechanisation further reduced the need for agricultural workers, and workers had to become skilled at operating machinery as well as the traditional husbandry skills. Farm sizes increased. Until about 1985 the government gave every encouragement to farmers to improve their land and buildings with grants, supported by a large and well-informed agricultural advisory service. Machinery and tractors were becoming readily available, new species of cereals and grasses were developed to increase output, fertilisers and chemicals were improving yields and animal husbandry leapt forward.

Willie Reynolds of Penybont in his demob suit in 1946

Post War

In real terms, the cost of food from the farm gate was slowly but steadily declining and from about 1970 holdings of 30 acres or less were no longer viable. To stay profitable more land had to be farmed, so farm size increased. In 1979 the Milk Marketing Board stopped collecting milk in churns. Farmers had to install a bulk refrigerated milk tank and many dairy farmers stopped producing milk. Within our parish very few of the farms in milk in 1945 produce milk today.

Many of the smaller farms rent out their land and others are '*hobby*' or life-style farms.

Coal lorry operated by the Evans family from The Plash

Railway closure

The railway continued to be busy until the 1950s when road transportation was deregulated. A decade later many branch lines closed following the Beeching report, including the line through Llanfallteg. Railway employees left to seek work elsewhere and houses in Llanfallteg became empty. In 1976 many were boarded up. It looked deserted and the village hall was derelict. No.3 Glenview was roofless.

No 3. Glenview derelict in about 1985

Village Revival

In the 1980s the village became a sought after place to live. The older properties were attractively priced, repaired and modernised by new owners, and a number of new houses and bungalows have been built. Employment for most people is out of the village and all families rely on a car, most have two. Agriculture is in the doldrums, employing few people, with few larger working farms. Farms are diversifying to attract tourists: former barns, cowsheds, stables and out buildings have been converted for holidaymakers and land has amenity use, particularly for horses and fishing. Several horse events are held in the village during the summer. Fish and the otter are back in the river.

The population of the village is similar to that of 200 years ago, whilst in the same time span the population of Wales has risen fivefold from 600,000 in 1800 to just under three million today. The growth in population has come in the cities, with people migrating away from rural areas to find work and escape the gruelling lifestyle. The village population reached a nadir in the 1960s, before recovering to some extent as people came to enjoy the benefits of living in a rural village without the drawbacks of life without modern amenities.

In the early 1980s, there were only three children in the village and Welsh was by far the predominant language. Recent arrivals have anglicised the village and it is difficult to hear Welsh spoken today.

Thanks to Welsh lessons at school, the majority of children can speak Welsh.

Life expectancy at birth has risen from Victorian times to 2001 from 44 to 75 for men and 47 to 80 for women. Now there are as many people aged over 60 in the village as those under 18. In 1881 children out-numbered the over 60s by three to one.

Mike Powell, a regular holiday visitor now retired to Llanfallteg.

Without modern drugs and because of poor hygiene, ten percent of babies did not celebrate their first birthday (compared to less than half of one percent now), and it wasn't until the 1920s that the infant death rate started to decline.

Nowadays villagers come from all over the UK. In 1881 virtually everybody was born in the local area, and only seven people were born outside Wales. The most popular names were Mary, Margaret and Elizabeth for girls, and Thomas and John for boys. Once, there were four clergymen living in the village and nearly all names were biblical ones; the Celtic names that are more fashionable now were noticeable by their absence.

The village is vibrant once again, thanks to the new Millennium Hall, modern utilities, easy transport and the disposable incomes of commuting villagers and retired people who appreciate a rural community life.

Source

Soper, Mike. *Years of change.* Farming Press, 1995.

LLANFALLTEG WEST

The small parish of Llanfallteg West lies to the west of the Tâf and it is here that the parish church, St Mallteg's, is found. Maps since the early 19th century show that a cluster of settlements has long stood near the church. The parish tithe map shows that Lletherllwyn Farm stood just to the west of the churchyard. Lletherllwyn was rebuilt in the early 20th century and renamed Llanfallteg House. Llanfallteg Farm stood on the eastern side of the churchyard. These properties are still present, although boundary changes, some name changes and new buildings mean that there is now a small hamlet adjacent to the church.

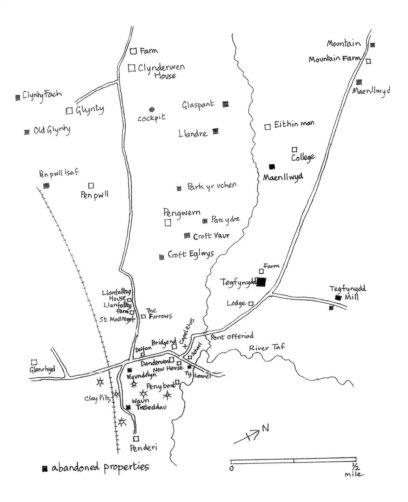

Llanfallteg West – early 20th century

St Mallteg's church

Another cluster of settlements has developed since the early 1800s closer to Llanfallteg Bridge and the river Tâf. Other farms in the parish include Penderi, Penpwll and Pengwern.

Penybont c. 1905

The Old Church Schoolhouse, also known as *Ysgoldy Goch*, and Dandderwen were both built in the northern corner of '*Brickyard Moor*', which takes its name from the former brickworks that stood nearby. Penybont Lodge has now disappeared and two modern houses stand close to its site. There is now no sign of Waundelyn. Immediately opposite '*Brickyard Moor*' stood Ty-bach now known as Delfan and this was reputed to be a drinking place.

Llanfallteg Church Room, c. 1986, Ysgoldy Goch

The Old Church School (Ysgoldy Goch) was constructed at the northern end of the '*Brickyard Moor*' and brought the first formal teaching to the village. It fell into disuse, and by 1980 there were numerous ash trees growing out through the back roof. However the building has been painstakingly recovered using much of the original material in the recent past and is having a second lease of life as a very pleasant home.

Pembrokeshire County Council established the Llanfallteg County Primary School 200 metres away from the Ysgoldy Goch, on the opposite side of the road. When the boundary changed back in mid 1950s, Carmarthenshire found itself with primary schools at Llanfallteg and Henllan Amgoed and consequently Llanfallteg was closed. George Adams, a corn merchant who lived opposite at Tâf Alaw, purchased it and used it as a store for many years. It is still standing and looks in reasonable order.

The County school

As with the eastern part of Llanfallteg, the decline in farming caused a fall in prosperity which was furthered when the railway closed until the 1980s. Since then it became fashionable to become a commuter or to retire. Many new developments have since taken place, and many on a size and scale that dwarf some of the old cottages in this rural community.

One benefit that the '*West*' did receive over its Carmarthenshire partner, was the rural electrification that arrived on the Pembrokeshire side, courtesy of the Cambrian Power and Light (CPL) Company network that operated in Pembrokeshire. With its two power stations, one in Haverfordwest and the other at Rushey Lake in Saundersfoot, CPL provided the first power to Llanfallteg in the 1950s. However it took nearly ten years before everyone could be connected. This was at the time of the post-war nationalisation of utilities and The South Wales Electricity Board sent out the first bills. The electric light had come to the darkest west!

In contrast to the Carmarthenshire side of Llanfallteg, the coming of the railway had a less marked effect, with no significant development arising as a consequence although there was a shift of employment away from the land. There are many local dwellings constructed around the turn of the century with bricks from Goodwick and Ammanford in particular. No doubt these bricks came in by train.

Glanrhyd

Contrary to many reports that the Romans came no further than Carmarthen, there is a Roman road which passes through the Glanrhyd grounds. In 1909 and 1913 children from Llanfallteg School visited the site and noted the importance of a '*very historical place*'. There are also reputed to be the remains of Stone Age hut circles in one of the Glanrhyd fields, known as Parc-yr-eglwys. Furthermore, the central pier of the gateway to the barn is a 2 metre monolith, all of which points to Glanrhyd being built on a very early site.

In 1600 Hugh Parry was one of the largest landowners in the area. When his daughter Ann married Arthur Wogan, the Castell Dwyran estate became part of her marriage settlement but Ann and Arthur sold the Plas Glanrhyd to Evan David Morris in 1630 and in turn he granted it in trust to David Lewis of Henllan as a post nuptial settlement on his heir Evan and his wife Joan.

John Evans was born in 1642 at Glanrhyd. He was born of wealthy parents, well educated and married to Lleucu. His father and two elder brothers died young and consequently the estate passed to him. He became converted to the Baptist faith and settled at Llwyndwr in Llandissilio. At his own expense, in 1701, he built Rhydwilym Chapel and in addition he gave Tirbach Farm nearby to the Church for the use of the Rhydwilym ministers. In his will, he made Griffith Howell a trustee for his children and his grandson, Evan Griffiths, who erected a monument to him at Rhydwilym.

On John's death, his son Owen succeeded to Glanrhyd and, as he had no issue, the property went to his sister Joan (Joanne) who had married John Griffith. When she died in 1776 aged 86, she was still living in the house. Her son Evan then became the next owner. He was appointed a J.P. in 1760 and High Sheriff in 1766.

During his lifetime he extended the buildings at Glanrhyd, including the threshing barn on which there is an inscription '*Thefe Barns were built by EVAN GRIFFITH Efq 1778*'. Above the inscription there was a clock. The clock was taken from its place on the wall by the young squire of Trewern. He and the son of Henllan wanted to marry a daughter of Glanrhyd and they fought one of the last duels in Wales in front of the house for her hand. The squire of Trewern won, and the clock is believed to be in Trewern to this day. The barn interior is much as it would have been when it was built, with its roof trusses still intact and ventilator slits visible.

Glanrhyd threshing barn

Glanrhyd sits on the southern edge of the sand belt. Unlike the clay soils further to the north, it made for excellent ceral growing. This threshing and storage barn was one of the first of its type in our area. It is quite unusual in that it has two pairs of doors each side. Most barns of this type had only one large pair of doors making loading and unloading of carts easier. The area between the sets of doors is also used as a threshing bay and winnowing area. The Glanrhyd barn predates the famous New Brownslade Model Farmyard at Castlemartin by 20 years. The Brownslade barn has only one very large access point either side of the centre bay of the barn (east and west). It was part of the Cawdor estate.

A year later when Evan Griffith became High Sherrif, he also built the office – again there is an inscription to the effect that '*Thefe offices were built by Evan Griffith Efq 1779*'. Evan was also said to be the '*Steward to Lady Dynevor's Court Leet for the Lordship of St Clears*'. The entrance is on the side of the building, and the room is not large. It has a window to the front, moulded fireplace, lime washed walls and an intricately painted ceiling. There are two panelled doors, one leading to the next room and the other to a stairway.

Glanrhyd Office ceiling.
©Crown copyright; RCAHMW.

The cart shed is on two floors, with no windows on the ground floor but three large doors. In the rear walls there are three ventilation slits. There is a wide external staircase leading to the upper floor. Here there is a window, an old butter churn and a windlass. Set back from but adjoining the cart shed, the entrance to the rear of the building is what is described as '*a short passage with corbelled roof beneath the staircase and adjoining a round-headed entrance to a cell or recess*', which was supposedly connected with the hangings said to have taken place at Glanrhyd.

In 1807, Glanrhyd and Pentroydin were leased between David Lewis of Henllan and James Morris of Pensarn for a period of eight years. Thomas Jones was farming there around 1818 for some time but by 1850s John and Rachel Morgan were farming the 281 acres with their son and daughter.

Offices and cart shed at Glanrhyd

John and Elizabeth Davies farmed there at the turn of the century with their five sons, Daniel 27, Robert 14, Caleb 22, Samuel 13 and Albert 8 and two daughters Hannah 24 and Elizabeth 14.

In the 1917 Gower estate sale Glanrhyd is described as '*a stone and slated farmhouse, four upper rooms and on the ground floor three rooms, kitchen, large dairy, churning room and kiln room with a cowhouse for 26 cows, small stable, large 60ft barn, calves' shed, cow house, stable for four and loft over part, large open cart shed, loose box, calves' cot and store with two large granaries over, two piggeries and open timber shed, rear enclosed courtyard with a well house together with 149 acres'*. It was let to Mr J.J. Howells at a yearly rent of £250.

The Glanrhyd Offices on the left with the old Farmhouse showing the wing added in the 19th century

After this sale there was a mortgage granted to John Henry John of St. Kennox in Llawhaden, a farmer. The Johns stayed at Glanrhyd until the late 1990s when the lands were sold off. The offices, farmhouse, barn and main outbuilding are all grade 2 listed. The Offices and the field around it were sold to Sue and John Cranmer who have plans to renovate the whole building. The larger of the outbuildings had been converted into a residence by Dai, the last of the Johns and this was sold together with the threshing barn to '*Ramjam*' and Ruth Silverstone. They sold the conversion on and are slowly transforming the barn into another home.

Penderi

Penderi used to be a farm off the main Llanddewi Velfrey to Llanfallteg road. In the past it was generally spelt as *Penderry*.

The first known owner of Penderi was Richard Parry, who was renowned as one of the obstructive characters of Llanfallteg's past. He owned and occupied Penderi during the 1600s and is rumoured to have had 21 children.

Penderi

On the 3rd May 1634, he was called to appear before the Court of High
Commission, relating to a disturbance he had created at St Mallteg's
Church, causing the sexton to apprehend him. On another occasion, he
had risen after the sacrament, exclaiming *'some devil is in my knee'*
and he said to the then rector, Roger Phillips, *'I am a better preacher
than thou'* and *'I care not a straw for thee'*. He also said of the
Archdeacon of Carmarthen that he hoped *'he would be hanged and if
he were king there would be no bishops in the land, but every Doctor
should have £100 per annum and every Master of Arts £20'* adding
'What good do Bishops do in the land?' He was ordered to make a
submission to the Church and in the Cathedral Church of Carmarthen
he was fined £2000, which was later reduced to 1000 marks.

Richard claimed that *'Arthur Wogan and James Price on June 23rd
1634 had insulted and ill-treated him with swords, staves and knives
and imprisoned him'*, for which he claimed £100 damages.

The Court met two months later and confirmed the fine of £2000 for
disturbance of divine service and profane speech, but his fine was
commuted to 1000 marks (a mark was worth 2/3rds of a pound). By
November it was proved that Richard could not pay the fine and a
commission was sent to Sir Richard Perrott and others, to take

Richard's bond with two sureties for £200. Richard was imprisoned at the Tower Chamber in the Fleet for non - payment of the fine.

On 20th November 1638, four years later, Richard petitioned the courts, highlighting his long imprisonment, great poverty and disability. The court, pitying his misery, referred his case to Doctors Duck and Eden.

However one year later, in 1639, Richard was still imprisoned in the Tower Chamber at the Fleet. His estate had been wholly seized. His wife and some children had perished for want of food, and he and the rest of the children were afflicted with such extreme poverty that they relied on the charity of anyone willing to help. He was now 74 years of age and for the last five years had '*lain on the boards and only had the alms of his chamber fellows towards his relief*'. He was not able to attend the courts, as poverty prevented him from seeing a solicitor to look after his business and so he was ready to die. The Court did not want him to perish in prison and referred the case to Sir John Lamb.

Richard died at St Giles without Cripplegate and his will was proved on 23rd April 1649. He was 84 years of age.He must have relented in his battle with the church as he bequeathed to the church of St Mallteg's 3s. 4d. and another shilling to St David's Cathedral His lands were left to his son Thomas, as well as a list of debtors to whom he owed money from the years when he had been imprisoned.

One of Richard's descendents was Rear Admiral Sir Edward Parry 1790-1855, known as '*Parry of the Arctic*'. He made many expeditions to the Arctic, including searching for the Northwest Passage and had the Parry Straits named after him.

There is a gap in our evidence for Penderi of some 50 years thereafter. By the 1720s, Penderi was in the possession of Phillip Howell, owner of the Castle Dwyran estate. In 1732, Phillip and Joan Howell of Castle Dwyran, along with Morris Griffiths of the Clynderwen Estate, were parties in the marriage settlement of John Howell and Jane Willy. Penderi, as well as Penybont and Wauntrebeddau and other properties in the area, plus '*oxen, bulls, cows, heifer, calves, ewes, lambs, sheep, pigs, goats, poultry, corn and grain*' were given to them on their marriage.

John Gwynne of Penderi is recorded as Churchwarden of St Mallteg's church in 1751. Edward John of Penderi was Churchwarden in 1762, and he was still at Penderi when he became Churchwarden again in 1774.

There appears to have been another change in occupier soon after, as in 1779 Evan Matthias of Penderi paid a land tax of £1. 12s. 6d. for Penderi and £1.10s. 0d. rent for the slang in Penderi, to John Parry, the owner. In 1786, Evan Matthias is named as the Churchwarden. In 1791, John Parry paid land tax of £4.12s. 2d, along with John Harding of Pengwern; well over half the total sum for the whole parish.

From 1806, Richard Hughes was living at Penderi. He was the son of 70-year-old Reverend John Hughes, who had served as rector at St Mallteg's for 40 years. Richard lived with his mother Celia and Elizabeth Harry, probably his grandmother, who was living on her own means. They had three servants, Mary Evans, Mary Morris and Margaret Matthias and three agricultural labourers, Daniel Thomas, Evan Rees and David Perkin. In his will of 1886, the Reverend Richard Hughes left £300 and a sum of £600 in a local property to meet local educational needs. Until 1895 the interest on this amount was paid towards the National School. Later the sum was applied to scholarships for Whitland Grammar School. The Hughes family were still there in 1841 during which time Ryce Jones owned the 81.2 acres of Penderi and the 20.2 acres of Penybont. The slang in Penderry Ucha was owned by William Parker Howell and occupied by William Lloyd.

By 1851 and until 1881, when he retired, William Lloyd was farming the 81 acres at Penderi. He died in 1891 and his son John, born around 1849, took over farming the land. In turn, on his death in 1910, his wife Mary Ann Lloyd continued farming. When she died in 1925, their son, Evan Bowen Lloyd and grandson John Howell Lloyd continued the family tradition of farming at Penderi until 1981. The Penderi estate was sold in 1863, including Penybont and Wauntrebeddau. In 1864, these properties were listed in the will of Miss Sophia Thomas. In 1903 the estate changed hands again and was advertised for sale in April, 1904 as follows:

Penderry: Situate in the Parish of Llanfallteg containing 80 acres or thereabouts, for the most part rich pasture land and now in the occupation of Mr John Lloyd, as yearly tenant, at the annual rent of £125, the landlords paying tithe 1903 value £9.14s. 3d. The farm is well watered, and the building comprise dwelling house, cart house, stables, 2 cow houses, barn and sheds. There are two small pieces of land intermixed with Penderry with boundaries undefined belonging to other owners. These pieces for which the tenant pays £1.10s. per annum are not included in the sale.

Wauntrebeddau: Situate in the parishes of Llanfallteg and Castledwyran, in the Counties of Pembroke and Carmarthen, containing 20 acres or thereabouts of excellent well watered pasture land and now in the occupation of Mrs Hester Williams, under a lease for 21 years from 20th September 1890, at the annual rent of £28. The buildings in this lot comprise a dwelling house, stable, barn, cow house, cart shed etc. The landlord pays the tithe 1903 value £1.5s. 10d.

Penybont: Situate in the parish of Llanfallteg containing 24 acres or thereabouts of pasture land now in the occupation of Mr Thomas Rowlands under a lease for 21 years, from 29th September 1902 at the annual rent of £40 and 3 acres or thereabouts of woodland in hand. The buildings on this lot comprise, dwelling house, cow house, barn, stable, piggeries, cart shed etc. The landlords pay the tithe 1903 value £2.19s. 5d. and under the terms of the lease allow £3 a year for 2 years more, as herein stated.

The three above lots will first be offered in one lot, adjoin each other and form a very compact estate. There is excellent trout, sewin and salmon fishing in the River Tave, which bounds the property for a distance of about a mile and a half.

Around 1980 the Boucher family bought the farm and kept a dairy herd here. The clay pits, used for extraction of clay for the brickworks which were dangerous to both man and beast, were filled in.

In 1998 the Cooks bought the farm and built up a business called Penderi Pine, importing furniture that they marketed from the former cowshed. It made an excellent show and sales room. In 2007 they relocated the business to Whitland but still reside in the house. The farmland has been sold and the barns are being converted into houses.

Penybont

Thomas Harry and his family had been living at Penybont from 1802. Penybont was a hamlet of 5 cottages, a mill and a lodge, also known as Ty Cornau. One villager, Willie Reynolds, remembers the walls of the lodge still standing in 1917.

Anne John outside Penybont Lodge c. 1900

Penybont Lodge also known as Ty Cornau – situated at the east side of Llanfallteg Bridge. There is very little evidence now of its existence other than a hollow in the ground, masses of daffodils in spring and domestic hedge plants in the corner of the field.

Thomas Rowlands moved from Carno, Montgomeryshire to the village to work as a railway platelayer. He took a lease for the 20-acre farm for 21 years from 29th September 1902, at the annual rent of £40 including 3 acres or thereabouts of woodland in hand. The buildings were a '*dwelling house, cow house, barn, stable, pig sties, cart shed etc. The landlords pay the tithe 1903 value of £2.19s. 5d, and under the terms of the lease allow £3 a year for 2 years more*'. After Thomas died, his wife Margaret continued to live at Penybont.

Thomas Reynolds moved into the property in 1918 with his family from Maenllwyd, just past College. They kept eight shorthorn cows and one workhorse here, which daily took the milk churns in a cart to Llanfallteg station. His son Willie still lives at Penybont.

Penderi Mill

The only remaining evidence of a mill here is the leat, which shows that the mill would have been of the overshot type.   In 1779 Cicely Morris left £3 to Elizabeth David of *Penderry Mill*.

By 1841 John Harry, aged only 15 was the miller.   Also living there were Sarah, 20 and Benjamin Harry, 13, presumably his sister and brother.

In 1851 the miller was Morris Morgan aged 35 who lived there with his wife Margaret, aged 39 and a servant by the name of Charles Thomas, aged 15.   Morris was still the miller in 1871 but his wife is now listed as Rachel aged 57 and he also employed an errand boy, James Evans (14) and a female servant, Margaret Perkins (17).

By 1881 the mill was no longer operating and the census recorded it as uninhabited.

Wauntrebeddau

Wauntrebeddau was associated with Penderi from at least the early 18th century. It stood immediately to the west of Penderi, and is shown on 19th century maps. It was put on the market with other Penderi properties in 1904, but disappeared from the landscape by the late 20th century. There is a small field close to the drive with a pile of stones where the cottage once stood.

Wauntrebeddau could mean the *'meadow of the three graves of the township'*, but no trace of any graves has been found. There is a story that there are nonconformist graves on the land of Wauntrebeddau. These were said to be the graves of Quakers buried around 1685.

Maybe the name was Waun trybeddi – *'meadow of the trivets or tripods'*. Trivets were used by weavers, or for drying hides, although it seems feasible that they were racks used for making bricks.

Waundelyn

A local tradition says that Waundelyn was built as a *Ty Unnos*. Neighbours, family and friends would all help to build a *Ty Unnos*, which according to tradition had to be started and completed between sunset and sunrise and have a fire smoking through the chimney by the morning. These buildings were squatter settlements, built by the rural poor, usually on common land or poor ground. Rough wood, turf and mud would be used in the construction, with rushes used for the roof. They were not intended to last long, but could be improved and extended if the builders succeeded in being allowed to stay on the land they had occupied. In the poor accounts of the village in 1826, £4. 1s. 2d. was given to repairing Waundelyn.

New House; Bont

The ground on which New House stands is also part of the field called Brickyard Moor, at Penybont, Llanfallteg. On the 4th November 1871 a 60 year lease from Robert Frederick Gower and Captain Erasmus Gower, his eldest son, gave a covenant to build a house and blacksmith's shop to *Thomas Evans of Llandysilio, blacksmith.*

The plot was 60 feet wide varying in length from 97 feet to 157 feet. A rent of £1 was payable half yearly. Thomas had to build on the field within one year, at his own expense and at a cost of £80, a dwelling house and smith's shop. He also had to show Gower's agents the receipts and bills and '*at the like expense scour, cleanse and keep in good order and repair all the sinks and privies belonging to the buildings.*'

In 1881 Thomas Evans aged 30, a blacksmith, is recorded in the census as living at '*Bont*' with his wife and seven children, the eldest aged 10 and the youngest only one month. This was undoubtedly part of the smithy. By 1891 the property is called New House. Thomas and his wife were still living there with five sons and three daughters in

1901 at number 1 New House which by then had grown and divided into numbers 1 and 2. Enoch Davies, a mason, and his wife Mary lived in number 2.

More modern council records show these as being New House and Pretoria, but the two were joined together to form one larger dwelling in the late 1980s.

Llanfallteg brickworks

Llanfallteg West sits on a boundary between a line of sand and gravel and the more typical clays found in the north and east sides of the community. The presence of clays in the area is shown on the 1891 Ordnance Survey map which shows a series of '*Old Clay Pits*' in a field known as '*Brickland Moor*', to the southwest of Llanfallteg Bridge. Late 19th century maps show that this field was harp-shaped, and was responsible for the name of the now lost cottage of Waundelyn (literally Harp Moor), which stood at its southern end.

The horse-powered Pug Mill in common use during the 19th century for mixing the clay prior to it being moulded into bricks ready for firing.

Brickyard Moor was purchased by the Gower family in 1825. Bricks would have been made on demand rather than it being a factory type business. During this time the Gowers were building the new additions to Clynderwen House and they may have started the brickworks just to supply their own needs. In later times when Tegfynydd was rebuilt after the fire, there was undoubtably a requirement for more bricks. Brickworks were often owned by local farmers or estate owners. They used their own labour force to either work in the fields or the brickworks, as the numbers required to run a brickworks was fairly minimal. The landowners could bring in extra labour from their estates at busy times. After the railway came to the village, some houses were constructed from brick for railway workers although most of the early ones were from slate and stone. It is most likely that these were moved down the construction trackway for the railway or from Glogue quarry.

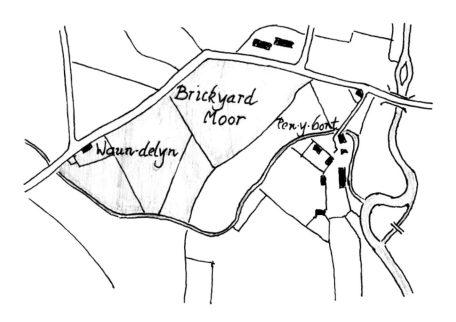

Brickyard Moor

Surviving invoices and orders, kept at the National Library of Wales, dated to 1841 and 1862, show that the brickworks at Llanfallteg was indeed producing pipes and bricks. From January 1841 there is an invoice for over 2000 2-inch pipes and 300 3-inch pipes. In 1862, John Evans from Clynderwen was engaged to operate the brick works and informed Mr Gower that the Llanfallteg brick kiln had discharged 25,000 bricks – enough for two houses, suggesting that it was a relatively large operation. The typical Llanfallteg brick was thin by current standards being only 2 ½ inches thick.

The old church school was made of local bricks and was called '*Yr Ysgol Goch*' or The Red School after the colour of the bricks in the walls. Many schoolchildren had, over the years, carved their names into the bricks and, during the refurbishment of the school to convert it into a dwelling in very recent years, some of these signed bricks were used in the construction of the outside walls. School records also state that the clay pits were frozen over during the winters and village children would skate on them.

According to the current owners, Tâf Alaw was the last house to be built using these bricks in 1935, the same year that the brickworks closed.

Llanfallteg Farm

In front of St Mallteg's Church stands Llanfallteg Farm, which is known to have been in existence since at least 1777. It was considered to be part of the Pengwern estate and may have been included in the settlement of the Castell Dwyran estate in 1657 on the sons of Elizabeth Gwynne, the owner and widow of John Gwynne.

The farm is next mentioned in 1789, as being part of the Pengwern estate, when Theodophilus Rees was renting it for £5.10.0d. yearly from Thomas Wildman, Barne Barne, John Harding and the Hon. Edward Bearcroft, the owners of both the Pengwern and Clynderwen estates. Theodophilus was Churchwarden at St Mallteg's Church in the years 1759, 1771 and 1783 during which years he was occupying the farm. His gravestone in St Mallteg's contains the inscription *'Departed this life, 18th December 1788 aged 61. Elizabeth his wife 21st April 1793 aged 63 and Benjamin their son 3rd January 1796 aged 49.'*

At the time of 1841 census, Thomas Roberts aged 30 farmed here, along with his wife Ann 30 and children, Margaret 11, Mary 9, John 8, Llewelyn 2 and Keturah John, a servant of 13. Also living here at this time was an agricultural labourer named Evan John, aged 43, with his wife Mary 30, and children Owen 10, John 7, Evan 4 and Gad, aged 2 months.

The tithe schedule of 1843 lists the farm as being in the ownership of the Gower family, where it remained until 1917. The land had increased to 41.3 acres and Thomas Roberts still farmed as a tenant.

In 1871 John Evans, aged 42, was farming all of 70 acres with his wife Mary 41, and son John, 16, along with 3 servants, James Howells, 49, Rachel Matthias, 22, and Ann Stevens, 10. By 1881 the farm had increased to 160 acres and John, now 52, was still farming with his wife, son and three new servants, Hannah John, 19, a dairymaid, Mary, 19, and Edward Matthias.

Mary Evans, aged 70 was farming with her son John in 1901; with them lived William Llewelyn, a carpenter of 18, Martha, a housemaid aged 22 and Martha Owen, 14, a servant.

John Archer Evans took over farming in 1910, but four years later the farmer was Josiah Richards.

In 1917 Captain Gower sold his Clynderwen estate, including Llanfallteg Farm. The sale details described it as a

'capital stone and slated house, adjoining the road and containing on the upper floor – 3 good bedrooms, small bedroom and large lumber room, on the ground floor, two sitting rooms, large kitchen, small kitchen, and good dairy. Brick shed, open shed and coal house. The farm buildings… arranged round a large yard, brick and corrugated meal house, brick and slated loose box, and cowshed for 5, calves' cot, cow house for 7, open cart shed, three stall stables, cart house and barn with loft over, cow house for 16 and calves' cot, two pigsties and fowl house together with several enclosures of good pasture land.'

This amounted to 77 acres 2 rods and 28 poles, in addition to which was the cottage Ty Bach. At this time Miss Richards paid a rent of £159 per annum.

SOUTH WALES

IN THE COUNTIES OF

CARMARTHEN AND PEMBROKE

Within a short distance of Clynderwen and Narberth Stations (G.W.R.), about 18 miles from Fishguard and 15 miles from Tenby.

The Particulars, Plans and Conditions of Sale

OF THE VALUABLE

FREEHOLD PROPERTY

KNOWN AS

The Clynderwen Estate

IN THE PARISHES OF

Llandissilio, Llanfallteg, Castelldwyran and Llandewy Velfrey,

Comprising a MODERATE-SIZED RESIDENCE and Appurtenances,

FOURTEEN COMPACT DAIRY FARMS

With Farm Houses and Buildings, known as

Clynderwen House and Home Farm, Cross Cottage, Penbrwynen, Clynty, Penpwll, Pengwern, Llandrefields, Upper and Lower Park Clovers, Llanfallteg, Pen Park, Glanrhyd, Tir Eglwys, Pentroydin, Altipistill and Cillefawr.

And several Small Occupations, the total Area being about

1,618 acres

Let to responsible Tenants and producing a present Rental of

£1,983 per annum.

For Sale by Auction by Messrs.

DEBENHAM, TEWSON & CHINNOCKS

J. S. RICHARDSON, R. M. SANDERS, F. C. CLARKE and W. J. DODDS)

IN CONJUNCTION WITH

MR. JOHN EVANS

At the DE RUTZEN HOTEL, NARBERTH,

On Thursday, the 7th day of June, 1917

At 2.30 o'clock, in 14 or 22 Lots,

Or in such other Lots as may be found convenient.

John Nicholas bought the farm at this sale. His children Morgan, Nesta, Ceinwen and May all went to the local Llanfallteg School.

John died in 1953 and his son Morgan took over the running of the farm. Morgan married Phoebe Edmunds and they had one child, Mary. He still had a pony and trap in 1989 in which he drove Veronica Woodford, daughter of Peter Woodford of Tegfynydd Farm to St Mallteg's Church for her wedding.

Nesta, Morgan and Mary Nicholas 1926

Morgan Nicholas sold land to Govan Davies for a quarry in 1990, but a forceful petition in the village stopped the quarrying starting. There had been some quarrying nearby over a century ago, as an old quarry is shown on the Ordnance Survey map of 1891, at the roadside opposite the farmhouse. A larger disused quarry also exists at the edge of Parc Chwarel woods, again to the north of the farmstead. The farmhouse remained empty until 1993 when Vivien and Paul Collier arrived.

Llanfallteg Farmhouse

Llanfallteg Farm - the old barn 1993
(V & P Collier)

Llanfallteg House; Lletherllwyn

This property was known as Lletherllwyn during the first part of the 18th century, but was referred to as Llanfallteg House in the census records during the 19th century. An agreement made in 1700 shows that Hector James, his wife Mary and daughters Mary, Margaret and Rebecca lived there.

On the 6th September, 1732 Phillip and Joan Howell of *Castle Dazzan* (Castell Dwyran) and Morris Griffith of *Llandysilio* agreed a marriage settlement between John Howell and Jane, daughter of Richard Willy, on the lands of Lletherllwyn and Ffynnonbrody, along with oxen, bulls, cows, heifer, calves, ewes, lambs, sheep, pigs, goats, poultry, corn, grain and hay. John David was the occupier. He is shown in the St. Mallteg's Church register as the Churchwarden in the years 1751 and 1769.

A document for the recovery of lands with John Howell of Wern, second son of John and Jane Howell, and Margaret Howell the widow of Richard, along with Kedgwin James of Haverfordwest, was submitted on the 8th July 1806. Evan Thomas was at this time occupying the land and paying a peppercorn rent. John Howell mortgaged the farm with John Callan of Grove, Narberth, for a term of 300 years for £400 plus interest, payable on the 26th November 1812, also paying a peppercorn rent on the feast day of St Michael the Archangel. Another similar agreement was made between the two parties on the 6th November 1815.

In 1823, John Howell, still farming, made an agreement with William Evan, shopkeeper of *Pant-y-maen* in Llanfallteg *to sit and let a parcel of ground, part of the tenement of Lletherllwyn, called Rhose, already built upon, to hold for 99 years, at a rent of £1. 5s. 0d. yearly, the dwelling and premises to be built upon the land to be kept in good condition.*

John Howell died on the 21st June 1825, leaving Bryn Maen, Llandissilio to his son Richard and Lletherllwyn to his son David, who occupied and farmed the place until his death, when a mortgage of £700 was agreed for the farm, otherwise called Ffoeswathan, between John Callan and Richard Lewis and signed by David Howell's executors.

Ann Howell took over the 71 acres in 1851 and ran it along with servants John Davies, Edward Lewis, Margaret Lewis and dairymaid Elizabeth Howell. In March 1852, Ann made an agreement with Margaret Evans of Bridgend to *'sit and let'* at a yearly rent of 10s. 0d. payable half yearly to hold for her natural life, and Ann promised to thatch the cottage in the forthcoming summer. In her will, Ann left all her property to her daughter, Mary, the wife of Henry Jones of Gilfachwen. An Inland Revenue account on 13th February 1875, addressed to Mary on the death of her mother shows the valuation of the farm to be £700, with a tax payment due of £90.

By 1891, William Howell Jones, aged 34, was occupying and farming Lletherllwyn, along with his mother, Mary, aged 66. They had several servants, Alice Tudor 19, Caleb Jones 24, Christine Lloyd 17 and Anne Rees 28, who was their house and dairymaid.

The old barn, Lletherllwyn

William Howell Jones stayed on as the farmer occupier for many years and in his probate papers dated 1932 - 1935 he left Bridgend House to Caleb and Ann James.

Mr. and Mrs. Thomas were there in 1949 and in 1954 Samuel Jones lived there.   Dr. Byron O'Neil and his family live there now.

Penpwll

Penpwll is a modified Welsh longhouse, originally built into a south-facing hillside on a sheltered slope, with windows along the east side only.   There were two cross-passageways through the house, from front to back.   The first of these runs from the present front door and ends at a large window at the rear, which was likely to have been a door originally.   The second remains, connecting a porch and back door. From north to south, the floor levels in each of the three ground floor rooms are lower than the next, in classic longhouse style.   Two doors in the house are reputed to be original.   They are made of elm and are of a simple design, with a few wide vertical boards nailed on to three horizontal rails, the hinges being a spike and hook system which enables the doors to be easily lifted on and off.

The house and farmlands were many years ago associated with, and owned by, Pengwern. The first reference is to Hugh Parry owning Pengwern and its surrounding lands in 1600. When his daughter Ann married Arthur Wogan, the farms and lands belonging to Pengwern were included in her marriage settlement, as they were again when their daughter Elizabeth married John Gwynne. When John Gwynne died in 1657, Elizabeth settled part of her estate, including Pengwern and Penpwll on her four children. Arthur was the only survivor and he took over the lands. He married Elizabeth Brigstocke and they had four children.

The next change of ownership, once again in the form of a marriage settlement, was when Phillip Howell settled the lands on his son John, and Jane Willy in 1732. At this time David John rented Penpwll. He had two sons, David born in 1716, and Roger who was buried in 1764, and his lessee was William John who died in 1777.

The ownership of the farm changed several times over the next few years and John Harding of Clynderwen House paid the land tax in 1791, with Thomas Paul renting Penpwll uchaf at £13 per annum, plus the house and garden and a piece of land at £2 per annum, whilst Owen John rented Penpwll isha at £12 a year.

John Howell became the owner during the early 19th century, but Pengwern and its lands were sold in 1825 to Abel Anthony Gower of Glandovan, Cilgerran. In 1841 Daniel Davies was renting 11 acres at Penpwll isha and also working as a carpenter. He lived with his wife Margaret, three daughters, Martha, Mary and Margaret and three sons Thomas, John and David. In the same year, Daniel and Rachel John and servants were farming the 58 acres of Penpwll uchaf. Daniel built the cart house and stables with bricks from the Llanfallteg brickworks. Alterations to the barn in 2007 unearthed a brick on which was scratched *'built by 7 8 9 10 and 11 Daniel John 1861'* – it is believed that the numbers refer to the months of the year.

By 1871, the acreage had again increased to 87 and there is no more mention of Penpwll isha. Daniel and Rachel continued to farm at

Penpwll well into the 1880s, building up the farm to 146 acres before moving to Fronhaul in Llandissilio.

Penpwll barn

In 1891, there was a change of tenant. Thomas and Hannah Davies farmed here, along with their children William, Caleb and Thomas and daughters Margaret and Annie, with two servants, Hannah and Elizabeth Beynon. Their son William became the first manager of Clynderwen Farmers Co-Operative, having first been a shopkeeper and postmaster in Llandissilio.

The tenants changed over the next few years. Thomas Howells and Joseph Merriman were here and, in 1909, William Williams was renting Penpwll and Clynderwen farm. His brother John joined him in 1910.

Penpwll was still owned by the Gower family until it was sold in 1917, along with other properties. On the sale details, Penpwll consisted of '*3 bedrooms, 2 sitting rooms, 2 kitchens and dairy, cowshed for 18, stable for 3 horses, cart house with granary over part, piggeries, hay yard and a garden, with 111 acres at a rental of £165 per annum.*'

John Davies bought the farm from the Gowers and on John's death in 1922, David Davies, Thomas Edward Davies, William Hughes Davies and Sophia Blodwen Davies sold the property to James Williams. James married twice; with his first wife he had a son, Benjamin who farmed at Bodau. His second wife, Ann, gave him at least four children: Elizabeth Ann, who died of a brain haemorrhage at 27; Hannah Caroline, who died at 30; Sarah, who married into the Eynon family and settled at Pengwern; John Thomas, who married Mary Ellen and farmed Penpwll.

James Williams bred and trained heavy horses for farm work. Shire horses stabled in the barn worked on Penpwll, Pengwern, Glinty and Clynderwen farms, all owned by the Williams family. The children of John and Mary Williams helped with the farm work from an early age. They had a favourite horse, a small cob called Polly, who pulled a trap on Sundays to Henllan Chapel. Polly was always used for pulling the '*pitcher*' during haymaking as she was so steady and could be relied on not to move unless told to. The pitcher was a kind of grab and, full of hay, it was pulled up swinging through the access door by the worker above in the hay store. The children played in the fields of Penpwll, especially the field below the farm called Parc y Pond, where the horses loved to roll in the water. Sadly the pond is now filled in. They also played in Parc y Barracks, which was the field below where the American army barracks were built during the Second World War, and in the ruins of Glinty issa.

Penpwll

By 1952, James Gerwyn Williams had been added to the electoral register for Penpwll and his wife Enid was added in 1958. In 1967, John Thomas Williams, living at Dolycoed, sold Penpwll to his son, James Gerwyn Williams for £10,000. He continued farming there until around 1990 when Stuart and Marilyn Soper became the owners. Penpwll was sold again in 1993, with just 10 acres of land, to Graham and Josie Hughes. They, in turn, sold it on in 2001.

Clynderwen House

Clynderwen House was possibly built on an earlier site, Klyn Derwen owned by Evan Griffith, yeoman. In 1634 he also owned Gilfachwen and assigned the house to Evan ap Eynon, yeoman. The Griffith family owned the Clynderwen House for the next 150 years. John Griffith lived there in 1712 and, on his death in 1726, it became the home of his eldest son, Dr Maurice Griffith, who married Barbara Phillips, widow of Richard Phillips of St Clears, the daughter of Henry Hensleigh of Panteague. Maurice died in 1725 and their son John took over the house. On 1st August 1764, he was party to a lease of nearby Pengwern Farm. He was also High Sheriff of Pembrokeshire.

There were many transactions, leases and mortgages over the next few years. Eventually, John Harding of Nelmes and his wife Sarah, who was the sister of Barne Barne of the Inner Temple, London bought Clynderwen House. Their son, also John Harding, sold the property in 1820 to Owen Evans Lewis and his wife, Elizabeth. Owen died the following year, aged just 22. His wife went to France leaving William Evans, who tenanted the farm, to keep the house in order. A comment in the sale after Owen's death states 'the house is elegantly furnished.'

The house with 760 acres was advertised in the Carmarthen Journal on the 11th January 1822 together with five farms totalling 1360 acres in all. In 1825 Abel Anthony Gower bought further land in Llanfallteg, and the immediate vicinity, for £4675. 18s. 9d. from Mrs Elizabeth Lewes. 'Clynderwen Mansion' was included in this sale, as were Glanrhyd, Pensarn, Tir y eglwys, Pentroidin and other local farms.

Abel Anthony Gower founded A.A. Gower, a firm of London merchants. Amongst other commercial interests he and his family had were investments in sugar plantations in Mauritius, which relied on slaves for labour.

He was one of 20 children (9 boys and 11 girls) of Abel Gower and Letitia, née Lewes. His grandparents William Gower Jnr, who was Mayor of Carmarthen in 1709, and his wife Jane, née Steadman, married in 1700. Jane's father, William Vaughan, had inherited Glandovan from his father. His ancestor Robert Vaughan built the house in 1579.

Clynderwen House in 1871

Admiral Erasmus Gower was a brother to Abel Anthony. He joined the Royal Navy in 1755 and in April 1804 he was promoted to Vice Admiral and appointed Commander in Chief, Newfoundland. Three years later he returned to England. He inherited Glandovan from his father but lived in Hampshire, where he died in 1814.

Abel died in 1837 and left his estate to his nephews Robert Frederick Gower and Abel Lewis. Robert inherited Glendoven and Clynderwen House, and Abel Lewes Castell Malgwyn. In 1860 Ambrose Poynter, a London architect, designed the extensions to Castell Malgwyn, and it has been suggested that he designed the alterations and re-built part of Clynderwen House, adding a grand Georgian façade of mellow red brick, probably made at the Gower owned brickyard in Llanfallteg. The arched vestibule led into a hall, 32 feet by 15 feet, with highly polished oak floors and carved oak sweeping staircase. The ground floor rooms included a billiard room, morning room and drawing room, and a further breakfast room, kitchen plus utility, laundry and cloakrooms. The slated cellars provided a wine store with 26 wine bins with a capacity of 1300 bottles and two further storage rooms. Upstairs as well as a master suite of two bedrooms connected by a dressing room, there were three other bedrooms and two large period bathrooms. The 17th century hall still had the original kitchen with an open Welsh chimney and the old ceiling meat hooks for hanging and smoking hams. The rear wing housed the dairy and four other rooms. There was a wealth of outbuildings, tack rooms and stabling with stone and slated barns and byres.

Clynderwen House with brick façade

After the rebuilding of the house, Robert Frederick Gower lived there with his wife, Lilias, son Erasmus and two daughters, Grace and Sarah, and during this time he acquired around 1700 acres in and around Llanfallteg bringing in a rental of £1572. 8s. 0d. per annum. He moved to Castell Malgwyn in 1876 and died there in 1884. In his will his estate was valued at £4061. 5s. 0d. He owned Glenrock Co. Ltd., the Chile Gold Mining Ltd., East Wheal Road Ltd., and Indian Consolidated Gold Co. Ltd. He owned shares in the South Wales Railway and the Swansea Vale Railway, and his son Erasmus was a director of the Whitland and Tâf Railway.

Clynderwen House (the oldest part is the wing to the left)

Once again the house saw a succession of tenants. It was advertised for a seven, fourteen or twenty one years' lease in 1889 in '*The Welshman*' along with 2000 acres of shooting. Erasmus Gower died in 1914 and was succeeded by his son Erasmus William Gower (1885-1958). He became a Captain in the 2nd Battalion, Royal Munster Fusiliers eight days before being captured at Etreux, France, in 1914 during the retreat from Mons. He sold the Clynderwen Estate by auction in 1917, whilst still a prisoner of war and many of the tenants bought their farms. The estate consisted of 14 farms totalling 1618 acres, producing an income of £1983 per annum.

After the sale the house was owned or rented out by numerous residents and it was taken over by the Ministry of Defence during the Second World War and used as a convalescence hospital for American soldiers and the East Lancashire Regiment also used part of the house as an officers' mess.

Mr and Mrs Lewis Thomas bought the house in the 1950's for £2,900 from William Owen and Mr Thomas became very well known as a specialist potato grower in the area. They lived there for well over 50 years until 1994, when the next owner carried out extensive renovations which were completed by 1999. The property was then sold again.

Pengwern

Pengwern is an old Welsh long house built into the hillside with windows along just one side. It has been altered many times over the years. Shown on the 1908 Ordnance Survey map of the fields belonging to Pengwern, was a cock-fighting pit. Cock fighting had been enjoyed for centuries but was prohibited in 1836.

Pengwern

The first traceable owner was Hugh Parry born around 1596. He gave Pengwern to his daughter Ann on her marriage to Arthur Wogan, one of 10 or 11 children of William Wogan of Wiston. Ann and Arthur had a daughter Elizabeth, who married John Gwynne of Piode, Llandybie and, on marrying, Pengwern passed to her. In 1739 Richard Gwynne sold the property to Morris Griffiths of Clynderwen and was a part of the Clynderwen Estate until 1917.

Ann Wogan (nee Parry) died young and Arthur Wogan married Dorothy, daughter of James Price of Abernant. They had a daughter Jane, who married David Lloyd. Arthur was a powerful and wealthy man and with his brothers John, Hugh and William owned 9 messuages (dwelling house with outbuildings and gardens) and 504 acres in Wiston, plus 92 acres in Llanychllwydog. With his brothers Hugh, Henry, William and Charles he also owned 50 messuages and lands in Lawrenny, Tenby, Yerbeston, Martletwy and the advowson of Lawrenny (the right to appoint clergy with a living to Lawrenny).

Arthur was involved in many court cases. In 1623, he was charged for non-payment of a dry goods bill for £3.7s.11d. In 1625, William Bowen sued Arthur for allegedly unjustly depriving him of some property. The same year, Ann, his first wife, disputed an inheritance with Jevan John Griffith, claiming that property belonging to her grandfather, Hugh should have been passed on to her via her father Henry Parry. Arthur was also at loggerheads with John Phillips over £100 due on a bond in 1629.

A year later, Arthur brought about more difficulty for himself when he attended a trial and caused trouble. In 1634/5 Arthur brought charges against Robert and Gwen Lloyd after they ejected his son-in-law, David Lloyd, from a property at Llanychllwydog.

Arthur's final case was in 1641 when James Lewis of the Great Sessions of Haverfordwest recovered £6. 2s.5d. from him. Dorothy Wogan was charged with recusancy for refusing to attend the parish church in 1637, although it is not known if she was a dissenter on religious grounds.

John Griffiths of Clynderwen became the next occupant in 1764. The house remained in the ownership of the Clynderwen estate, even though the tenants changed considerably over the next few years.

John Thomas was a tenant farmer here in 1776, paying a rent of £31. 9s. 0d, which continued until 1787. Samuel Morgan was also paying 7s. 0d. to rent a *slang* there. John was appointed Churchwarden at St Mallteg's Church in 1776 and again in 1808.

The ownership of Pengwern changed in 1779 when Richard Knethell, Rev. John Thomas and Evan Griffith bought the farm for £7105. It remained in the ownership of the Griffith family for several years. The following properties were recorded as belonging to Pengwern: *Parkydre, Parkdan Dandre, Croftyr Eglwys, Park yr uchen, Croftvaur, Penpwllisha, Penpwllucha, Pengwern, Llanvallteg.*

John Howell sold the house in 1825 to Abel Anthony Gower (1748-1837) of Glandovan, Cilgerran, Pembrokeshire although he continued to live at Glandovan until his death. The Gower family owned 242 acres including Pengwern, and this passed to Abel Gower's nephew Robert Frederick Gower, who lived at nearby Clynderwen House.

Rees and Martha Evans and their son Griffith, farmed 38 acres of Pengwern during the 1840s and 50s along with Evan John, an agricultural labourer.

In 1871, Esther Howells ran 67 acres, helped by her sons James and Peter, daughter Elizabeth, a dairymaid and two servants. One of these was a Benjamin Eynon, who later married Esther.

By 1891 a farmer named Thomas Jones farmed the property with his wife Margaret, and sons Joseph, William and John and daughters Elizabeth, Hannah, Letitia and Mary and a servant Henry Williams.

Owen Williams was in occupation of Pengwern by 1910, followed by Evan Howells in 1914. He bought the farm when the Gower family sold their Clynderwen House estate in 1917. The sale details show it to have '*3 bedrooms, 3 ground floor rooms and a kitchen, a slated cowhouse for 12, cart house, stable for 3, barn and chicken house and enclosures of 105 acres of pasture and woodland*'. Mr. Howells was already renting the property for £90.0s. 0d. per annum.

In 1926 the Eynon family were farming here. Sarah Williams, daughter of James Williams of Penpwll, married into the Eynon family and their children Rowland and Annie lived and farmed at Pengwern during the 1920-30s. John Thomas Williams and his wife Mary farmed Pengwern but lived at Penpwll. Chris and James Davies became the next owners of the property, selling it in 1988 and moving to Clynderwen village. The Palmer family then took charge.

Sources

Church records

Francis Green papers

Lewis, E. T., *Local Heritage from Efailwen to Whitland* ,1975.

Jones, Francis. *Historic Houses of Carmarthenshire and their Families*, Newport, 1997.

The Tegfynydd Estate

The road from Llanfallteg West towards Tegfynydd, crosses the bridge (Pont Offeiriad) over the Afon Rhydybennau. Legend has it that in 1792 a clergyman crossing the bridge fell out of his horse drawn carriage into the stream and drowned.

Passing Brynheulog and Nodfa, properties built around the 1930s, Tegfynydd Lodge marks the overgrown drive leading to the ruins of Tegfynydd Mansion.

Tegfynydd Mansion

The name Tegfynydd could be derived from *Teg ffin ith*, meaning fair river boundary, with the Tâf, Rhydybennau and the stream from Efailwen forming the boundary. It could also mean *'Fair Hill'* or *'Fair Mountain'* referring to the higher ground it sits upon.

The earliest written record of Tegfynydd is associated with the Norman baron William de Breose who held a vast area of land in south Wales from 1203 until 1208. It was subsequently confiscated by King John but redistributed to the family before 1216. Later it was probably part of Whitland Abbey lands.

With the dissolution of the Whitland monastery in 1539 the land reverted to the crown, which then leased out or sold the land. James Lewis of Abernant Bychan held a lease from 21st June 1594 for 21 years on much of the previous abbey lands around and about Llanfallteg. He died in 1598 and it is thought that his son took over the agreements.

During the 17th century Tegfynydd was sold to the Mathias family of Kille, Llandissilio, who were described as minor gentry. Arthur Mathias in 1664 owned a messuage and lands at Tegfynydd and sued Griffith Richard of Llanfallteg for ploughing up a road leading from Tegfynydd towards *'the Great Close and a tenement called Le Tithin mawre o'r tre'*. Arthur Mathias of Llanfallteg was buried on the 25th June 1697 at Llandissilio.

There is a grave in the churchyard of St Mallteg's, Llanfallteg, to John Mathias of Tegfynydd 1712-1771, with the following inscription:

'Behold, spectator, underneath I lye

It is my lot now, tis yours by and by'

The next family to live there was that of Richard Pritchard (died 1795), who was licensed by the Bishop of St David's to practice surgery in Narberth. In 1768 he constructed a new stretch of road 100 yards long between Tegfynydd and Llanfallteg. He married Cicely (died 17th February 1777) and their daughter Elizabeth was born at Tegfynydd.

On 15th November 1774 Elizabeth married John Howell in Llanfallteg. John was the eldest son of Thomas Howell of Ffynnon Felin, Llanwinio, and Anne Willy, originally from Lampeter Velfrey. Elizabeth's parents settled Tegfynydd, Upper Tegfynydd, the mill, a messuage in Llandissilio, and Redstone in Narberth, on their marriage. Probably the Georgian house was added on the south east side of the existing house on the occasion of the marriage.

Tegfynydd House
©Crown copyright; RCAHMW.

Elizabeth died and was buried on the 27th June 1785 at Llanfallteg. John married Mary Williams *nee* Phillips in 1786 and moved to Penrheol, Meidrim; a second marriage for both of them. Mary was previously from Llwyncarreg having married Rees Williams of Penrheol.

John and Elizabeth's son, also a John Howell, Doctor of Physic, resided at Tegfynydd in 1818. By 1829 he was described as a widower living at St Mary's Haverfordwest on the occasion of his marriage to Augusta Ince Webb Bowen at Camrose. He died five years later and is buried at Camrose. With no heirs the property was leased to the Rev John Hughes, rector of Llanfallteg, and his son. The occupants in 1841 were William Thomas, a minister, and also John Hill, a cleric, plus their families.

The Morgan family

On 26th June 1846, Dr John Lloyd Morgan M.D. of 33/37 High Street Haverfordwest bought the Tegfynydd Estate with its 302 acres from Thomas Brightwell for his country seat; included in the sale were the mansion and farm, Upper Tegfynydd Farm, mill, College, Maenllwyd, and Tegfynydd Mountain.

In 1857 he bought the adjoining Rhydwen Farm, Llandissilio from Mr Williams of Aberdare. This estate was 320 acres and included Llwynglas, Green Bush, Eithinman, Llaneiron otherwise Brynaeron, and Parcgwyn otherwise Rhos.

John Lloyd Morgan was born in 1793 in Haverfordwest, the son of Roger Morgan a merchant, and his wife, Jane. Another son, Thomas, was a solicitor, who in 1841 was living at Castle Square, Bridge St, Haverfordwest. Their sister Jane married William Stroud Esquire on the 13th August 1839, a banker, residing in High Street Swansea. The family crest was a stag's head *couped* at the shoulders; an *armed arm embowed* grasping a javelin. Their motto was *'fortitudine et prudentia'* (*'with fortitude and prudence'*).

With his father's mercantile connections John Morgan probably travelled by sea to Glasgow, and overland the 40-odd miles to Edinburgh University where he was educated. This sea journey would have been much more comfortable than the two to three weeks coach journey over poorly surfaced roads.

On the 2nd May 1820 John married Margaret Spear in Edinburgh, the daughter of Robert Spear. They moved to 33, High Street Haverfordwest, where he was a practising physician. Shortly after returning to Haverfordwest he arranged a lease on a building in St. Thomas's Green that became a Quaker Meeting House known as *'Green Meeting'* where their four children were christened.

After a marriage of some eleven years his first wife died and on the 8th September 1835 John Morgan, now 42, married 19-year old Eliza Sophia Starbuck at Steynton. In 1841 their daughter, Eliza Mary was born, followed by Mary Alice in 1844.

Eliza had been born in Pembrokeshire in 1816, the daughter of Paul and Mary Starbuck. Her grandfather Samuel Starbuck and Timothy Folger were the senior members of a group of approximately fifty American Quaker Whalers from Nantucket. They came to live in the new port of Milford and continued their business of whaling and producing whale oil that was used for lighting the streets of London.

Paul Starbuck hosted a dinner for the Anti-Slavery Society on the 16th July 1824. Selected affluent or influential guests, who were sympathetic to anti-slavery, were invited. John Morgan was there and he hosted a similar dinner the next night at his home in Haverfordwest. The guest speaker was Thomas Clarkson, who with William Wilberforce was a prime mover of an Act of Parliament passed in 1833 to halt all British involvement in the slave trade.

The residents at 33/37, High Street Haverfordwest in 1851 were John Lloyd Morgan, practising physician, his wife Eliza, and children Augusta, Howard (gentleman), Frances, Eliza Mary and Mary Alice. A cook, housemaid, nursemaid and coachman were employed. In later years John resided during the summer and autumn months at Tegfynydd, where he died on 19th October 1867.

In 1881 at the age of 65, Eliza lived in Charles Street, Steynton, her income being derived from land. She employed a cook, housemaid, parlour maid and coachman.

John Morgan was clearly very successful. At the time of his death in 1867 he owned at least forty properties that included small cottages, farms and town houses. His ownership of government bonds was greater than the capital issue of the shares of the Whitland to Cardigan railway, and he also had shares in the Grand Junction Canal. His will is very interesting because his only son Howard did not directly inherit any property, cash, bonds or shares but could use Tegfynydd during his lifetime and receive all the income from the estate. On his death Tegfynydd was to pass to Howard's eldest son, Christopher Hird Morgan. The other forty or so properties, bonds, shares, stocks etc were distributed to his immediate family. The daughters and widow were very generously looked after.

In 1856 Howard Spear Morgan married Annie Lloyd (1829-1867), daughter of Henry Lloyd, and they moved to Rhydwen around 1858. After eleven years of marriage and five children Annie died in 1867. His father died the same year and Howard moved to Tegfynydd.

The residents of Tegfynydd in 1871 were Howard Spear Morgan, JP for Carmarthen and Pembrokeshire, his two unmarried sisters Augusta and Mary Alice, children Edith, Lloyd and Catherine, along with a staff of governess, nurse, housemaid, cook, kitchen maid, coachman, and a gamekeeper. Tegfynydd Lodge appeared on the census for the first time. Phillip Neate, gardener and domestic servant with his wife and three children were in occupation.

Howard and Augusta gardening

There was a fire in the Georgian house and the family moved to Walcot in Somerset, taking the opportunity to remodel and extend the mansion. In 1881, the only people recorded at Tegfynydd were a housemaid and parlour maid plus two visitors - the brother of the housemaid who was a sailor, and his wife.

Howard's eldest son Christopher Hird Morgan (born in 1857), studied law at Cambridge and married Isabella Celina Elizabeth, daughter of Thomas Blyth, in March 1883 at Kensington. He was now a barrister at law living at 15 Philbeach Gardens, South Kensington, London, SW5, but had inherited the Tegfynydd Estate from his grandfather and was probably responsible for the rebuilding, with thoughts of spending the summers at Tegfynydd.

The architect is believed to be J. P. Seddon who was renowned for his work in the Victorian Gothic revival style. In 1860 he was the architect for the nearby church of Llanddewi Velfrey and also the Aberystwyth hotel that later became the University of Wales.

A large and imposing extension was added around the Georgian house. The main entrance to Tegfynydd was built of dressed native stone with Bath stone facings in the Gothic style, that opened into a very fine galleried entrance hall with tessellated pavement and a huge hooded fireplace, lit by a skylight in the vaulted roof. The drawing room was 24ft by 18ft, library 20ft by 15ft, and dining room 29ft by 16ft 6in, all with plate glass windows. A handsome stone staircase led to the eight principal bedrooms, two having dressing rooms adjoining and there were two well fitted hot and cold bathrooms and two WCs. There were also five bedrooms for servants plus servants' hall, kitchen, scullery, butler's pantry, larder, storerooms, and WC. In all there were 52 rooms and 365 windows.

The new railway and sidings in Llanfallteg made transporting large quantities of Bath stone and other materials to the building site, which was only a mile away, relatively convenient.

Tegfynydd fireplace

Floor in Tegfynydd

By 1883 Howard Spear Morgan (59) had returned to the recently refurbished Tegfynydd with his 2nd wife Elizabeth (30), born in Cheshire. In 1891 Howard and Elizabeth were still at Tegfynydd, along with their daughters Gwenllia aged 6 and Lorine 5, plus a nurse, under nurse, housemaid, parlour maid, cook, and groom /coachman.

On the 28th July 1894 Howard died and on the 12th February 1898 his eldest son Christopher (41) also died, leaving his wife Isabella to inherit the Tegfynydd and Rhydwen estates.

Christopher Morgan '*was taken ill on Wednesday last with acute influenza and expired on Saturday morning death being due to the failure of the heart's action.*'

The Haverfordwest and Milford Telegraph also had a report of Christopher's funeral in the 23rd February 1898 edition, stating: '*The funeral of the late Mr Morgan of Tegfynydd took place on Wednesday. The remains were conveyed from London by the mail train arriving at Clynderwen at 6.0. a.m. on Wednesday morning. A hearse was provided to convey the corpse from there to its last resting place in a quiet corner of the Llanfallteg churchyard, alongside the grave of his departed father. The coffin was of massive polished oak and heavy fittings and the plate bore the inscription "Christopher Hird Morgan B 1857 D February 1898. A very large number of beautiful wreaths and crosses of flowers were placed on the coffin and tenants of the estate – about 30 in number – each bearing a wreath, walked in procession all the way in front of the hearse, and a large number of sympathetic neighbours and friends followed. The bearers were selected from among the tenants and old workmen of the estate. At the entrance to the churchyard the curate in charge Rev. Mr Lewis was accompanied by the 'late' aged vicar the Rev W Evans of Lan. The churchyard was crowded to excess and the service truly impressive.*'

There is a memorial in St. Mallteg's church.

'Sacred
To the Memory of
Howard Spear Morgan J.P., & D.L.
of Tegfynydd
Who died on the 28th of July 1894

*This tablet is placed here by
the special desire of his eldest Son
Christopher Hird Morgan M.A. Cantab, & J.P.
who died on the 12th February 1898'*

In 1910 Kenneth Walker leased the mansion and the hunting and fishing rights for 14 years. He was related to the Walker whisky family and was a keen hunting, shooting and fishing man. George Griffiths from College was groom from 1912 -1914 and has recorded that the stable yard included 5 hunters, 4 race horses, 1 polo pony, 1 harness pony, Shetland pony, donkey, a colt and a filly.

At the back of the house a pony, parrot and dog are buried and a headstone remains with the following inscription:-

*'Joey
Dear old faithful friend
b 18th November 1899
d 4th August 1913'*

Mrs Walker showed an interest in the village school and regularly held Christmas and Guy Fawkes parties for the children in the main hall of the mansion. An entry from the school logbook on 23rd September 1915 states *'at the request of Mrs Walker children marched to the railway station to meet 10.45am train to give a reception of some wounded Australian soldiers'.*

Estate dispersal

An auction sale of part of the estate that excluded the mansion was held at the Yelverton Arms, Whitland on 28th July 1911 when *Eithin Man*, *Pen-i-Fai* and *Rhyd-wen* Farm were sold.

John Evans auctioneer from Cardigan held a sale of the remaining Tegfynydd estate on the 24th September 1920 at the Yelverton Arms for Mrs Isabella Morgan, who was then living at Drayton Gardens, South Kensington.

Details from the sale document describe the house as a modern and well-built country residence approached by a carriage drive, with luxuriant shrubberies on either side containing many fine specimen trees. The ornamental grounds covered four acres with a fine lawn in front of the house, plus a conservatory. An acre of walled fruit and a kitchen garden with three heated glasshouses were behind the house. There was also a fruit room for the produce from the well-stocked orchard of an acre and a quarter.

The outbuildings consisted of five stalled stables, harness room and large coach house, two loose boxes, wash room, cart horse stable, cart houses, dog kennels, cow house with five stalls, calves' house, fowl house and runs.

George Griffiths was present at the auction and recorded that there were no bids for the mansion and 32 acres. The mansion and the farm comprising 143 acres were then put up for sale together, but withdrawn at £8,500. The mill and three cottages on the estate were sold.

However, in 1921 Major Morgan Jones, Lord of the Manor of Pendine, bought the mansion, selling it again in 1936 to John Maurice Thomas, a local auctioneer.

One of his sons is living in Clynderwen and lived at Tegfynydd as a young lad until the army commandeered the house in 1941. He remembers a grand house with a beautiful mosaic floor in the hall, the only other similar floor being in Manchester Central Station. In one of the bathrooms was a vast bath carved out of a solid piece of slate. The attic held a large water tank with water coming from springs just south of Bronydd, some one mile distant, and piped through cast iron pipes. The pipes were at least 18 inches deep and men with picks and shovels would have dug the channel part of which was through rock.

The garden was a feature with a beautiful shrubbery and, in the spring, a mass of golden daffodils lined the drive from the lodge to the house. The walled kitchen garden and orchard were so productive that surplus produce was sent by train to London. In front of the house was a croquet lawn. One winter during the war some of the large oaks were cut down and dragged over the lawn, turning it into a mud bath.

The Ministry of Defence acquired the Pendine Ranges in 1941 and Major Morgan Jones with his wife and son were moved from their home, Llanmiloe Mansion, Pendine to Tegfynydd.

Major Jones was a magistrate and well known for riding around the lanes in a gig drawn by two grey ponies even though he had a car. His son Gwyn married and at one stage of his life lived at High Grove, now the home of Prince Charles. Willie Reynolds from Penybont recalls that tragically Major Jones shot himself in a dressing room at Tegfynydd.

The Times obituary report stated: '*On 4th July 1943, suddenly, at Tegfynydd, Major Morgan Grainger Jones, late of Llanmiloe Pendine*'.

Tegfynydd was sold again to the daughter of Dr Saunders who converted the house into two flats. Captain Houghton and his wife occupied one. Brigadier Llewellyn Alston and Metta, his wife, occupied the other from 1954 to 1962. The Brigadier was a churchwarden at St Mallteg's and kept hounds at Tegfynydd. Metta was the last person to live in Tegfynydd.

In 1962 the mansion house and 4 acres were for sale. Relatives of the earlier Morgan family considered purchasing the property. It was in a poor state. Lead had been removed from the roof, the timbers had a fungus, and an architect advised them to pull the house down and start again. Eventually it was sold to the Reynolds family who made enquiries about renovations. An estimate in excess of £100,000 to return it to its former glory was beyond them and, like so many other country houses, it was stripped of its fine furnishings and left to nature.

The mansion and 4 acres were for sale again in 1989 by auction at the Nantyffin. People came from far and wide to view the property including a contingent of Japanese people to see if it would make a golf clubhouse in Japan. Eventually it was sold to the Woodford family who were living in Tegfynydd farmhouse.

Tegfynydd Mansion and farm in 1967.
(skyviewsarchives.com)

Unfortunately it needed no makeover for an appearance in the film Hedd Wyn as a ruined French Chateau. Hedd Wynn was a Welsh farmer's son who, whilst serving in the army in France during the First World War, wrote the winning entry for the chair at the 1917 National Eisteddfod at Birkenhead. Sadly, Hedd Wynn was killed in action in the battle for Pilckern Ridge in Ypres on 31st July before the Eisteddfod was held; he was awarded the chair posthumously. The film was made in 1992.

An article by Sheila S. Thompson, a relative of the Morgan's, that was printed possibly by the Western Mail in 2001 entitled '*Just a Heap of Childhood Memories*' ends with '*it is slowly dying on its feet – or rather, foundations*'. Now the once beautiful house is a ruin but has been replaced with a modern bungalow just below the croquet lawn and life goes on.

Tegfynydd Farm

The house and farm buildings lie to the North of the mansion. About 1841 the farm was approximately 205 acres of pasture, 65 arable acres and 6 acres of woods. Cows, cattle, sheep and horses were kept, all requiring a considerable workforce to tend them. Single workers were usually housed around the farmstead, perhaps sleeping over the stables. It was usual for the farmer's wife, with the help of servants, to feed these workers. There were five cottages on the Tegfynydd estate for married farm workers and their families. The miller's cottage was opposite the mill; the other four cottages were at the northwest end of the estate.

Maenllwyd Cottage housed a sawyer and his family, with the use of 5 acres of land. Nearby College had a large ¾ acre garden. Two cottages were at Mountain, one with ½ acre and the other with ¼ acre. All three housed agricultural labourers and their families.

By 1881 Tegfynydd Farm was 120 acres occupied by Thomas Evans (72), his wife, and their 29-year-old unmarried son. Two male farm servants, one female general servant and a dairymaid were employed. Maenllwyd by College no longer existed but had been replaced with a new property also called Maenllwyd, built near to Mountain in a field named *Parc Cerrigllwydon Ucha*. Isaac Phillips, an agricultural labourer, and his wife occupied the cottage and 7 acres. There was only one cottage at Mountain, with 14 acres of land, occupied by Ddu Phillips, a tailor, and his wife.

Forty years later Tegfynydd farm was 147 acres with a large farmhouse, cow house, stables and numerous out buildings including a dovecot. At the 1920 auction of the estate tenants had the opportunity to become property owners although the farm was not sold. The tenants in occupation of the mill farm and the three cottages bought their properties.

Peter Woodford and family moved from Buckinghamshire to Tegfynydd Farm in the 1970s. Peter was an enthusiastic farmer and true countryman. He kept cows, beef cattle, grew corn, (ground by a small electric mill as the water mill was closed), bred pointers, reared pheasants, and also wrote a book 'Born to Farm', recording his memories. When he retired he moved to the bungalow at the foot of Tegfynydd. His son Jeremy lived in the bungalow called Jayswood on the opposite side of the mansion.

Today no corn is grown but cattle and sheep graze the fields and occasionally a pheasant is heard, one that has escaped the shoots and the fox.

Tegfynydd Mill

The Mill is reached by going straight over the council road from the farm.

Water corn mills were in existence in the eleventh century and were mentioned in the old Welsh Laws by Hywel Dda. In the early part of the nineteenth century there were probably at least 100 mills in Carmarthenshire. An increase in population created a growing demand for flour, but with the repeal of the Corn Laws cheaper and better quality wheat arrived from North America, Russia and Australia. With the grain arriving at sea ports, mills were built nearby, enabling the corn to be milled on site and then distributed more conveniently as flour. In 1854 Joel Spiller opened a steam-powered mill in Cardiff. With ever more importing of good quality cheap grain, especially wheat for bread making, the mills around the docks flourished and were constantly modernising. By the early twentieth century most were using rollers instead of millstones. Transport from the docks was made easier with the railway and then later roads, making it very difficult for the local traditional mills to compete. As the grain merchants increased their businesses, farmers turned to buying their stock feed from them with specially formulated blends and the demands for the local mill diminished, leading eventually to closure. Farmers continuing to grow corn for their stock and used horse, tractor, or stationary engines to power their own small roller mills.

Tributaries were frequently used to power mills, as the flow of water was adequate. The main river was likely to flood so requiring substantial building work. The stream to power Tegfynydd mill rises at Efailwen entering the Tâf near the Plash. About three miles from the source was a fulling mill at Felin Cwrt, which was mentioned in the Castell Cossan Grange inventory of property under the control of the Cistercians. Today it is a private house. 600 meters further down stream a millrace was dug, diverting the water to a millpond with a sluice gate thus controlling the flow of water to the overshot mill at Tegfynydd.

The earliest written record of this water corn gristmill is in 1774 as part of a marriage settlement when the daughter of Richard Pritchard of Tegfynydd married.

The mill is a substantial stone building, built in three stages from around 1800 onwards. The moist grain, mostly barley and oats, would have been crushed for cattle feed. Wheat and some barley would have been finely ground and then sifted to produce flour. These grains needed to be very dry and a fire, with grain drying floor above, was located in the east end of the building. On the west side of the first floor the dry grain would have been stored ready to be lowered onto the grinding stones. A bread oven was to the right of the fire.

On the 28th July 1911, part of the Tegfynydd estate was for sale and Lot 1 was '*Felin-Teg-Fynydd or The Mill Farm*'. The land amounted to 35 acres and the farmhouse consisted of '*a parlour, kitchen with range, scullery and dairy, with two bedrooms on the first floor. The mill was described as an excellent water corn mill of two floors fitted with water wheel and three pairs of stones, hydraulic elevator, barn with drying floor, cow byre with seven ties, cart hovel, two pig pounds and small stable.'* Mr David Thomas was the tenant on a yearly Michaelmas tenancy at an annual rent of £66, with fishing rights in the river Tâf. The property was not sold until the 1920 Tegfynydd sale when Mr Thomas Thomas, the tenant, bought the property for £1,900.

The mill remained operational for another 15 years, finally closing in 1935. Many tracks leading to the mill that would have been busy with horse and cart, or pony and donkey with panniers strapped to their sides taking the corn to and fro, are still in evidence today. The millers' house and out buildings are heaps of rubble, while the mill building, paddle and driving wheels, millstones and oven remain. Planning permission to change the use to a residential dwelling has been granted.

Tegfynydd Mill

College Farm

According to local legend, College was a school for the children of estate workers. John Mathias (1712-1771) of Tegfynydd left two guineas to be paid annually for a schoolmaster to teach five poor children. The cottage was on the Tegfynydd estate and beside an ancient estate track that led from Tegfynydd to Llandissilio.

In 1841 John Davis, an agricultural worker, his wife Margaret, and their three children aged 13, 9 and 1 occupied the cottage which had a large garden of ¾ of an acre. At the bottom of the garden was another cottage, called Maenllwyd with 5 acres. Ten years later Maenllwyd was not listed in the census and College had taken over the 5 acres. Until recently there was a very large boulder near to the site of the cottage.

Dan Perkins, a labourer, and his wife and four children were the residents in 1871. Dan had changed employer as he and the family were at Ty Bach (now Delfan), a cottage on the Pengwern estate in 1881.

In 1881, Martha Thomas, a widow and annuitant aged 57, was listed as the occupier, with her daughter Mary, aged 17, who was a dressmaker. Mary married Edward Griffiths, a railway plate packer. In 1891, Edward, aged 26, lived there with his wife, their son Dewi, aged 5, and mother-in-law Martha Thomas.

At an auction in 1911, the cottage was described as having '*two rooms downstairs with a small dairy on the ground floor and 1 bedroom over, with a good garden and 5 acres in five enclosures. Water was obtained from a well, and the property was let on a yearly tenancy of £8 to Edward Griffiths*'. The property was not sold until a sale in the 1920s. After being a tenant for almost 40 years, Edward Griffiths, with his son George, bought the 32-acre smallholding for £500.

George wrote many notes recording significant events in his life and fortunately the family has kept this information. He was a keen horseman and '*had a situation as groom with Mr. K. Walker at Tegfynydd from October 1912 to 29th September 1916*'. His next employment was for Sir Owen Phillipps at The Kennels, Travellers Rest, Carmarthen, where he worked as a groom from 1st October 1916 until 24th June 1917. On 1st July 1917 he started work at Penllwyn Farm, Bethesda, where he was rehired on 10th October 1917 for '*£28 and grazing for a ewe*'.

George Griffiths 1917

George, with Edward and Mary.

On 15th October 1918 he was hired for £50 to work at Great Vaynor, Clynderwen, but returned to Penllwyn Farm on the 18th October 1919, hired for £80 and the keeping of a ewe. In 1920 he was hired to stop on again at Penllwyn '*for £100, a weeks holiday, and a few odd days off*'.

He recorded in his diary that on the 10th October 1921 he sold a ewe to his brother Owen who was at Pengwern. Prior to returning home to College on 18th October 1921 he bought a shearing machine from the Dyffrynconin sale for £28 10s 2d.

George kept cows, sheep, pigs and horses at College. In 1925 he married May Anne Davies and they lived at Yet Fawr, Login and then later at Bryn Hill, Clynderwen. In 1928 George bought a 12-acre field adjoining College, thus increasing the size of the holding to 44 acres.

With the outbreak of the Second World War, College responded to the challenge to increase food production. Britain had very low stocks of food and fertilizers and only 35% of food consumed was produced in Britain. Five acres at College were ploughed up for barley.

Victory Churn Contest
(1944~45)

This Diploma is awarded to the Farmer & Farmworkers of *Brynhill farm, Clyn derwen* in the County of *Pembroke* in recognition of their loyal work for their Country in its time of need. The milk production of this farm showed average milk sales for the whole herd of not less than two gallons per cow per day throughout the winter period.

Diploma for average milk sales of not less than two gallons per cow per day over the winter period in the Victory Churn Contest awarded to George and May Griffiths at Bryn Hill

George's son, Hugh, was chairman of the Clynderwen YFC in 1945 when the club restarted after being in abeyance since 1936, due to the general depression of the 1930s and the Second World War. In 1953 Hugh married Jennie, a farmer's daughter from Cardigan whom he met on a Young Farmers inter-club visit. His new bride came with some cows - a wedding gift from her family.

From 1954 George kept a daily diary recording significant farming and family events, with Hugh carrying on from 1959. George and Hugh farmed Bryn Hill and College using College for dry cattle, hay, corn, potatoes, swedes, mangolds and kale.

Mary died in 1954 at the age of 90, having lived at College for at least 73 years. George, May, Hugh and Jennie decided to leave Bryn Hill and move to College. Before moving over in 1955, they raised the roof on the cottage to make three bedrooms. The farmyard was built with cowshed, dairy, feed room, hay barn and midden (manure store).

The cows were Friesians and the milk was collected from the churn stand at the top of the drive until 1976 when a bulk tank was installed. The cows were often taken to Tegfynydd to the bull although there is an entry for a calf sired by the Eithinman bull (next door), though it is not noted if it was planned or if the cow escaped!

Later the hay barn was modified to store silage and College became one of the first farms in the area to make silage. Battery hens were kept, with a van from the Clynderwen Co-op calling to collect the eggs. George had kept pigs from his early years and he continued to do so at College. The sows were taken to a boar at various local farms with the pork sold to the Clynderwen Co-op or at local marts.

A Case tractor, which was originally built in the USA in 1943 and imported by the UK government, was purchased. It spent its early life in Scotland before coming down to Wales and College in the 1950s. Around 1980, it was restored and is often seen at vintage shows in the locality exhibited by its Pembrokeshire owner.

Hugh Griffiths and tractor

Understanding the needs of farmers, Hugh canvassed the immediate farming community to ascertain their requirements for electricity. He did so from 1950 after the Labour government had issued a policy statement that electric power would be made available to all in the rural areas. Hugh never let those in office forget their political commitment and regularly wrote reminding them there was still no power in this area. Electricity eventually arrived on the farm in 1959. Mains water arrived from Rosebush reservoir at a similar time and a two-storey extension with kitchen, bathroom and a fourth bedroom were added to the house.

On Saturday 8th September 1962 Hugh recorded in his diary that his wife and daughter 'went to Cardigan by rail on occasion of closing the passenger train, last train travelled today'.

Both George and Hugh were progressive hard working farmers and dedicated to improving the farm, even though when Hugh was young he had thought to be a pilot. The family was always taken to the annual air show at Brawdy.

George and May retired to Myrtle Cottage in Clynderwen in the 1960s. Hugh, Jenny and family moved in 1977 to Llandissilio after four generations and approximately 100 years of occupying the holding.

In 1978 Mike and Heather Bearman, with their two daughters, were the new occupants of College Farm. They came from an aviation background but wanted to start a dairy farming business. At that time the farm was 45 acres with a cowshed for 14 cows, dairy with bulk milk tank, hay/silage barn and midden with channels enabling the effluent to drain to the nearby stream, and several corrugated iron sheds.

The aim was to concentrate on one enterprise only and that was selling milk. The cow shed was changed to an abreast milking parlour to milk eight cows at a time; a cubicle shed, concrete silage pad, and slurry tank were erected and 16 acres of land nearby was bought. Most of the fieldwork was carried out using contractors, but two tractors were kept, one for scraping the yard and another for feeding out the silage.

Forty pedigree Friesian/Holstein cows were the start of the herd, which increased gradually. The first cow to calve was called Milkshake who later produced triplet Holstein heifer calves all of which grew into useful members of the herd. The milk was collected daily by the Milk Marketing Board bulk tanker and taken to the creamery in Whitland where a machine to turn milk into butter oil was installed in 1991, making the creamery the most modern in Europe. Much to the horror and dismay of the local community the creamery was closed shortly afterwards.

Cows on the road near College

As the herd increased the business became profitable, but all the facilities in the farmyard had to increase. In 1989 the farmhouse was extended yet again, this time adding a utility room, shower room, another bedroom and double garage.

In 1994 the dairy herd was dispersed and in 2006 the house was sold with 18 acres. Over 200 years the property had changed from a 5 acre holding to the centre of a 200-acre farm, and now it is an 18-acre pony stud holding.

Sources

The Friends of Narberth Museum. *Remembering Slavery,* 2007.

Jones, Francis, *Historic Houses of Carmarthenshire and their Families*, Newport, 1997.

Lewis, E. T., *Local Heritage from Efailwen to Whitland* ,1975.

Mike Soper. *Years of change.* Farming Press, 1995.

Sale documents of Tegfynydd held by HJ & MT Bearman.

LLANFALLTEG EAST & THE VILLAGE

Around two hundred years ago the east end of the modern village was a small collection of dwellings at a crossroads on the junction between the main road through the village and a now partly lost road which ran from Rhydywrach, north-westwards through a ford on the Tâf and on towards Tegfynydd and Tegfynydd Mill. This small collection of houses is named as Rhyd-ddol-esgob on early maps. The name is significant as it refers to the '*Bishop*'s *meadow by the ford*' and is quite probably an echo from the days when the Llanfallteg area was a property of the Bishop of St David's Llawhaden estates.

The present road through the village was built in the early 19th century as part of the turnpike road network in the area. At the same time, the Llanfallteg Bridge over the River Tâf was constructed. There was a realignment of the road at the west end, with a new piece running in front of Bridgend House rather than to the rear, and also at the east end, where a new piece of road was constructed from Rhyd-ddol-esgob up to Llwyncelyn and Lan.

The bridge over the Tâf cost £461-19-4½ to build by David Parry and Thomas Thomas from Llangan, commencing in October 1808 and completed the following year. The bridge and new road formed part of the Narberth to Newcastle Emlyn turnpike. Tolls were collected in Llanddewi Velfrey and Llanboidy.

The current bridlepath from Rhy-ddol-esgob looks likely to have joined the existing footpath, which crosses the river behind the Plash Inn. This route was certainly in existence when the tithe maps were drawn up in the early 1800s, and a wooden bridge crossed the river. About 1966 the local authority replaced the wooden bridge with the current concrete one, and tried to copy the original with modern materials.

Construction of the railway and the station and platforms in 1874/5 had an impact on the cluster of houses at Rhyd-ddol-esgob. The new railway was laid through the heart of the settlement and a number of dwellings appear to have been lost as a result, based on the evidence of comparing the 1831 and 1891 Ordnance Survey maps.

The tithe map of 1843 shows where there was settlement on the south-eastern bank of the River Tâf near the ford. Only a small number of dwellings are shown where the village later developed, although Rhyd-ddol-esgob was, of course, a cluster of dwellings listed under the one name. Subsequent census records reveal there was little change until after 1871.

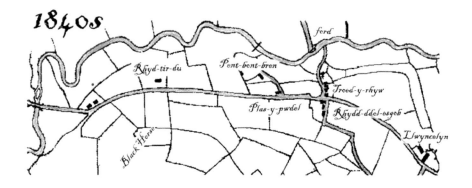

Llanfallteg East in the 1840s

The Black Horse was a new build, and was almost certainly constructed when the new river bridge was completed. In its early life it is recorded as being an Ale House. This building burnt down and was replaced by the current one, known as Taffside, but now named Dolycoed.

**Rhydtirdu, with Adams Street on right
(Later Adams Row) about 1910**

However, along the road lay Rhydtirdu, a traditional thatched Welsh cottage and at the time owned by the Thomas family. This holding was some 40 acres and stretched right up to where the railway was subsequently built. In the early 1900s, it was occupied by Amaziah Morris and family, who moved down from Penlan.

Amaziah was a big man in more ways than one. In many early village photographs he can be clearly identified standing head and shoulders above his neighbours. He was a Minister and he played a major part in chapel affairs.

The foundations of Rhydtirdu can just be seen in the field by the stream even now, and Morgan Siop recalls that it still had a roof on it in the 1950s. Almost opposite stands Adams Row (street), originally a terrace of three houses, built by Mr. Adams for his three sons around the turn of the century. They stayed in this form until the mid 1990s when the westerly house was incorporated into the centre one.

In 1820 the other known dwellings were Plas-y-pwdel (*'mansion in the mud'*) and Penbontbren. The latter is still standing after major rebuilding in 1986, sitting alongside the footpath to the river bridge. This was the only access to the main road until the gardens associated with the *'Plash Terrace'* were sold and a new drive was constructed to the road. Plas-y-pwdel lay just along the same path, and was renowned for being, yet another, ale house. This building was lost under the current public house and carpark, when the then Railway Inn was built towards the end of the century. In 2004, a new Plas-y-pwdel was constructed in the field behind.

However within ten years there had been a three-fold increase in the population here. This was a direct result of the coming of the railway, which brought key workers and their families into the area. Once the railway had become established, particularly after consent was given to run passenger trains, even more development occurred with new businesses springing up to meet the needs of those using the railway.

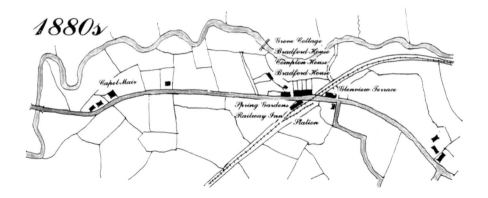

Llanfallteg East in the 1880s

Over the next forty years, Llanfallteg continued to develop. Home workers, such as knitters, tailors, blacksmiths and cobblers occupied many houses. They made their living by trading at the station, or actually travelling on the trains. There was a small increase in the number of dwellings, but life in the community remained fairly stable during this period until the outbreak of the First World War.

Compton House, along with Golden Key (also known as the Brick House, which suggested that it is a late addition) became the village provisions store. *'Siop Morgan'* sold almost anything and had its own bakery, which operated until the 1960s.

**Morgans shop,
now Compton House with Golden Key (Brick House) beyond**

In the early 1970s, David and Norleen Morgan reached retirement and the shop closed. The shop premises, which had utilised the whole of the ground floor and the upper floors were converted back into a dwelling house. The bakery and store were demolished and Golden Key was left to fend for itself and looked decidedly derelict by 2000. The two houses were then sold and new owners have since refurbished Golden Key back to its former glory and it has served as playroom, holiday cottage and overflow accommodation following the birth of twins Grace and Lilly born to Christine and Ian Young in 2006.

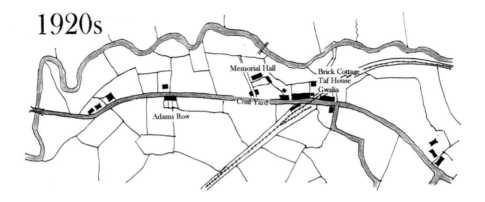

Llanfallteg East in the 1920s

From 1920 until 1965 there was another period of little growth or change. However, the village did acquire its first village hall brought in by Mr Adams from Aberporth. It was erected on the Memorial Playing Field and not surprisingly known as the Memorial Hall. It proved to be a popular meeting place and was well supported until the advent of television, but during the 1960s it fell into disuse and neglect. It finished its days as an inglorious motor repair shop, before being demolished in 1985 after being declared unsafe. A long legal tussle followed, and a new group of trustees took charge of the Memorial Playing Field and restored it back to a usable and valuable asset for the community.

The Memorial Hall about 1980

The year 1964 saw the railway close under the '*Beeching Axe*'. For a number of years previously more and more goods were being moved by road, people ceased coming for the trains and the local businesses suffered and closed down. Many houses were left empty and by 1975 some were derelict. When the railway came in the 1870s, it brought cash and prosperity into the community. Conversely, decline set in when the trains stopped running. Lewis's shop closed and the top three houses became empty and by 1975 they had a derelict air about them. Near the Plash, Spring Gardens and Hope Cottage suffered a similar fate.

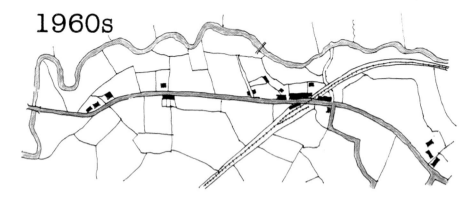

Llanfallteg East in the 1960s

A new phenomenon appeared at the end of the 1970s which revitalised the community, the young commuter. They moved into the old terraced houses, renovated them and bought the community alive again after some 25 years of decline. Progressively all the derelict dwellings were made good and currently all are occupied. By 1985 there were no more dwellings to renovate, so new bungalows appeared at either end of the village. Early ones were modest, but with increasing numbers moving in from more affluent parts of the UK, bigger and bigger mansion style bungalows have become the norm.

Until this time the community was predominately Welsh speaking, but it now had an ageing population and relatively few children and young people. Between 1980 and the present day the Welsh language has unfortunately disappeared almost entirely from the village, although it remains the language of education for many local children at school. The balance of ages has changed too, with the 2001 census showing almost equal numbers under 21, 22 to 60 and the over 60s.

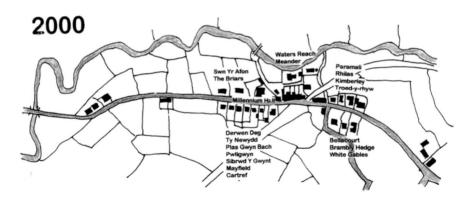

Llanfallteg East in 2000

More recently yet bigger homes have been built and occupied by mostly English '*escapees*' who have benefited from the difference in property values in parts of England compared with those here in the west of Carmarthenshire.

Village services struggled to survive the loss of the trains. The coal yard closed immediately. The pub survived, but the shops have all gone except the post office, which is open on two mornings per week. Mail still gets delivered to the door and there is also a daily collection. The National Lottery funded the provision of a new Millennium Hall, and the Memorial Playing field just behind, which still provides an outdoor recreational area for all to use.

Llanfallteg village centre

In 2008 there are 46 dwellings in this stretch of road, compared with 23 in 1901. The railway station has been demolished and replaced by three new houses, the centre one being named Golygfa'r Rheilffordd (*'Railway View'*). Rhydtirdu is almost lost without trace, but footings can just been seen, and a similar fate has befallen Blaenffynnon.

The Millennium Hall

The opening of the Millennium Hall

From left to right;- Richard Meade, Amey Richmond, Cllr Dia Thomas, Trelech, Cllr John Gibbon, Cllr Jimmy Morgan, Wyn Williams, Betty Adams, Bethan ACT, John Bodkin, Caroline Burford, Istyn Pynn, Earnie Goodrich, Dave Peterson

The Millennium Hall was constructed with monies from the National Lottery and the Millennium Commission, as a millennium project.

It is constructed on the former gardens of Spring Gardens, The Plash and Hope Cottage. At the end of 1980 these gardens lay side by side to the south-west on the end of the terrace, with Hope Cottage garden nearest the road, the Plash at the rear and Spring Gardens in the centre.

The Vaseys who occupied the Plash, for a short time also owned Hope Cottage, and at this time they sold both gardens to Pat Turton who owned Spring Gardens. An attempt to build a new house on these gardens was turned down by Carmarthenshire County Council. The furthest end of the garden was sold to make the garden at Penbontbren larger and also give direct access to the road. The piece in between was purchased by the Community Council.

Working with the newly formed Community Association and Antur Cwm Tâf, the Millennium Hall was built. It is a timber framed building built to a very high energy efficient specification, and has proved to be a valuable asset to the community.

The Plash Inn

The Plash Inn is the only pub to bear the name in the United Kingdom and the only business still trading on the roadside in the village

Plas y Pwdel is clearly shown on the Tithe Map of 1841 as being alongside the path from the footbridge over the Tâf and Rhyd-ddol-esgob. The best interpretation of Plas-y-pwdel from the Welsh – English dictionary is - '*The Mansion in the mud*' or '*Puddle Palace*'. It had the reputation of being a drinking place.

Census returns show that until 1871, there were up to three dwellings at Plas –y-pwdel, numbers 1, 2 and 3.

In 1841, at number 1, Mary John aged 80 was the owner and head of the household, living along with Rachel John, presumably her daughter, and grandchildren Elizabeth and Dinah. Elizabeth Adams aged 70, an independent pauper, lived alone at number 2. William P

Howell owned the 0.2 acres there in 1843, with David John occupying a field and a garden, with a tax of 6d due.

Rachel John was still living at number 1 in 1851, with her grandson Evan Owen. David Evans, an agricultural labourer, lived at number 2, with his wife Sarah and children Hannah and Rees. Hannah Thomas resided at number 3.

At the time the railway was planned, most of the land in this part of the village was part of the farm of Rhydtirdu owned by the Thomas family. The Evans family, who had strong roots in Fishguard, lived at Plas y Pwdel then bought some of the farmland, and on it constructed what is now The Plash. The 1871 census records that David Evans, his family and a boarder, Elizabeth Williams, were in Plas y Pwdel number 1. He became then owner of eight acres. His son Rees was a carpenter. A 79-year old pauper, Elizabeth Gibbon and her daughter Martha, a needlewoman, were living at number 2.

In the 1870s David Evans took advantage of the impending construction of the Whitland and Tâf Vale Railway, which started from Llanfallteg, and built 'The Railway Inn' and its neighbouring houses immediately adjacent to Plas-y-pwdel. By 1878, The Railway Inn and its farm of 13 acres was still owned and occupied by David Evans, now 59, living with his wife Sarah and Elizabeth, his 27-year-old daughter, who was a waiter in the inn. His son, Henry, also lived with them and later in 1881 he is recorded as being an unemployed railway engine cleaner.

'The Railway Inn' may well have been better known as 'Plas-y-pwdel' to locals in its early days. By 1881, according to local legend, it acquired the name 'Plash' from English or Belgian workers working on the rebuild of Tegfynydd Mansion, who were unable to pronounce the Welsh name and commuted it to 'The Plash'.

The Plash in 2008

The publicans in 1891 were young, 24 year old Rees Perkins and his wife Annie. His mother – in - law Ann Morris, a widow, lived with them. His niece Edith Morris was also staying at the inn. Penelope Evans, a milliner was living at Plas y Pwdel.

Henry Evans on the old wooden bridge over the river

By 1901, Henry Evans and his wife Catherine were the innkeepers, also farming the land with a servant, Mary Thomas and three sons, Gwilym, David and Jeremy. They stayed there until 1931 when Henry passed away. The Evans sons continued running the Inn with Jeremy Rees and Walter Gibbon over the period until 1963, with Thomas Henry being the last of the Evans family to be landlord.

Left to Right   MORT SALMON - WILL JENKINS - WILLY JOHN - ELFED GRIFFITHS - BERT BENNETT
GRANVILLE GIBBONS – EMLYN LEWIS – WINFORD EVANS – GODFREY BOWEN - GORDON PHILLIPS

Drinkers in the Railway Inn, 1957

He retained ownership of The Railway Inn until about 1965.
Thereafter a series of the Evans' family members inherited the pub
and farmland, and passed away in very short time. Reg and Stella
Nelson leased the pub for two years from the Evans family. Whilst
they were there a set of wooden steps was installed from the kitchen to
the room above, and they also did Bed and Breakfast for fishermen
who came down on the Tâf and surrounding rivers. The Nelsons had
three children and Andrew, the youngest, was born in the back room
upstairs during 1964.

The railway closed and The Railway Inn changed its name to The
Plash. John Thomas briefly succeeded the Nelsons. The Plash then
came into in the hands of Etta and Jack Fish, followed by Mike and
Mary Bentham, who ran it until 1974.

When they left Roy Williams, Ivy Blackmoor and Jim and Sheila Reynolds took over. During their time the Brewery Cottage at the rear of the pub was renovated and a new bar recovered from a tailor's shop in Whitland was installed.

A Londoner, Ron Mills then came in 1980 and kept the Plash for some 6 years, just as a drinking house.

A revolution came with the next owners in 1988, when John and Pat Vasey moved in and brought The Plash into the 20th Century, with modern toilets and food served on the premises. The steps in the kitchen were removed and in a bold move, John set up a Caravan Park in the paddock at the rear. For possibly the first time ever, Llanfallteg became a holiday destination, with many of those visitors still returning today to sample the unique features and atmosphere of the village and pub. Brewery Cottage was again renovated to bring it fully to current standards. Between them, the Vaseys and Ron Mills dismantled the farm by selling off the land, and new bungalows were built there during the succeeding years.

Jeff and Ella Beattie moved in after the Vaseys left in 1997. Jeff was a man with a strong military background and ran the pub the same way. The staircase to the upper rooms, previously hidden behind the door in the bar, was removed and replaced by an external steel staircase. The bar area increased but to the dismay of many regulars, the narrowing between the bar and staircase was lost. Together Jeff and Ella developed the pub whilst maintaining its charm, and rebuilt the outbuilding to create Swallow Cottage, in what had been the milking stalls and barn back in the early days of the Evans' occupation.

Jeff was well past retirement age when he called the day on being a publican, and ownership passed to the Goymer family with Steve and Christie behind the bar. They brought a younger face to The Plash, and have young children, something that had been missing there for many years. By 2003 the caravan park had disappeared and the land was developed for new houses, although the Brewery Cottage was still used for holidays and longer lettings.

Today The Plash retains many of its original features and has never been extended; the bar and the dining room are small. There is a log fire and from the beams hang jugs and pots. Steve and Christie made the place bigger by adding a loft extension. The owners, bar staff and the villagers maintain a warm and friendly atmosphere.

Glenview Terrace

Glenview Terrace was built during the 1880s, and stood immediately to the east of the railway crossing in Llanfallteg village. There were three homes in the terrace with the top one No 3, being built first, and the lower two added over the next ten years. Gwalia was added some 20 years later.

Glenview Terrace - 1910

In 1881 Edward Lewis, a shop keeper born in Llanglydwen, aged 24, lived at No 3, the top house with his sister, 22 year old Hannah, together with shop assistants and tailors, 21 year old Thomas Phillips, born in Llanboidy, and John R Davies aged 19. There are many photos taken at the turn of the century showing this to be a thriving shop. Siop Lewis continued to trade for many years selling hardware, clogs, and even motorcycles.

By 1891 David Lewis, also born in Llanglydwen, was a tailor and draper here, along with his wife, Sarah, aged 30 and their 4-year old son John. Phoebe Lewis also lived with them. She was 22 and a servant as well as a dressmaker. In addition they had an apprentice tailor, 14-year old James Davies.

David Lewis was still living at No. 3 in 1901 with his wife, son, and also a daughter, Maggie, aged 5. Hannah Thomas was their servant and David Davies, born in Llanfyrnach, aged 28, was a tailor living with the family along with two apprentices.

In 1985 when the current owners Billy Gardiner and Emer Furgusson moved in they found numerous bits and pieces from its past life including clog irons, bicycle and motor spares. The house has been renovated and the workshop in the rear turned into a comfortable studio flat.

At No.1, in 1891, George John and Henry Thomas, both rail workers, lived with a housekeeper, Briget John and her daughter. In 1901, William Edwards aged 60, a railway platelayer, lived here with his wife Miriam aged 49. Another railway worker David Roberts aged 50, lived with his niece Jane aged 28 at No 2. In 1901, Penelope Evans, a needlewoman of 60, lived there with her 40 year old daughter. These are possibly the two women outside No. 2 in the photograph.
By the early 1970s both these buildings were almost derelict. New roofs saved them from total collapse and by the end of the 1980s, Lyn and Karen Jones had renovated and lived in both of them.

Tâf House

Tâf House (also recorded as Taff House or Taff Cottage) stands some 100 metres along the old railway line from Llanfallteg Station.

When the railway construction started in 1871, the company had its workshops and engine shed in Llanfallteg. One of these workshops is thought to have been the forerunner to the dwelling that became Tâf House. Anecdotal evidence suggests that originally the building was a single storey carpenter's workshop for the railway constructors.

The land on which it stands is shown in the Tithe Schedule of 1843 as being in the ownership of the Thomas family who owned Rhydtirdu. At this time there were few dwellings in the location and the land was in agricultural use. Rhydtirdu land was evidently split up, no doubt at the time of the first building of the railway, and it passed into ownership of David Evans of the Railway Inn and Farm, a holding of some 9 acres.

The coming of the railway led to a rapid expansion in development around the station area and a complete change of lifestyle. Before the railway construction started there were only 5 dwellings listed in Llanfallteg East but ten years later there were 17, according to the 1881 census. Tâf House was not listed at this time.

The first evidence of Tâf House appears in 1886, when David Evans of The Railway Inn leased the parcel of land for 69 years to John Isaac, a timber feller then living at Llanfallteg Station. There is a covenant preventing *'converting any premises into a public house for the sale of beer or any intoxicating liquor'* during the term of the lease.

By the turn of the century, Llanfallteg East had grown to 24 dwellings. John Isaac's son David was now living at Tâf House with wife Ann and three children, his father and a servant. David is listed as being a tailor and draper, no doubt taking advantage of the coming and goings of passengers to the trains. He moved to Clynderwen and appears in the London Gazette with David Isaac going into receivership in 1907 *'formerly of Tâf Cottage Llanfallteg'*.

The next known occupier was James Morris, followed by Maggie Morgan by 1923. Ronnie her son was born there in 1924 and returned to live there in 1951 with his wife Jean. This was after war time service in the Royal Engineers as a driver. In between times, Owen Jenkins, Ernest Nelson and William Morris are recorded as living at Tâf House.

In 1935, the Whitland Rural District Council installed a reservoir on Gwarmacwydd lands, with water pipes of cast iron or asbestos running alongside the railway land to give Llanfallteg village its first mains water supply. Part of this pipework system runs beneath the present gardens. The asbestos pipe is still in use under the road supplying almost all the village down to Dolycoed.

The Evans family of The Railway Inn retained ownership until 1968, when it was sold to Ronnie and Jean Morgan. They further purchased a six-foot wide strip of land at the rear of the house from the Evans family in 1974 and subsequently extended the dwelling. The extension was so closely matched to the land purchased that the boundary fencing posts were nailed to the wall twenty years later!

Ronnie was a railway trackworker, and in 1974 he and his wife secured the ownership of some 270 yards of the former railway track together with a cattle creep. The Cardi Bach was of course, one of the first branch lines to close in the Beeching period, with trains ceasing to run in 1963.

Tâf House 2009

Ronnie retired in 1985, and Jean moved back to her hometown of Sutton on Sea to be with her mother. Ronnie reluctantly followed and Tâf House was sold. He made many return trips, but '*no more Welsh nails were going to be hammered into the house at Sutton on Sea*' he retorted on a train heading out of Carmarthen on one of his last trips back to Sutton-on-Sea. It was with great shock that the village learned that Ronnie had shot his wife shortly afterwards, was convicted and sent to prison. On release he returned to Wales and lived out his days in Carmarthen.

The current owner of Tâf House has been there since the Morgans left. He has been employed in electricity supply generation, and as such has been a medium- to long-distance commuter ever since moving in.

An 80-foot wide strip to create a rear garden was purchased from the owners of the '*The Railway Inn*'. The cattle creep and a short length of the former railway track has been sold to another neighbour.

In 1999, in the middle of a cold night, the house was destroyed by fire. It was rebuilt and from the outside looks very similar to the way it looked for possibly 100 years, but the inside was reshaped to suit the owner's needs at the time.

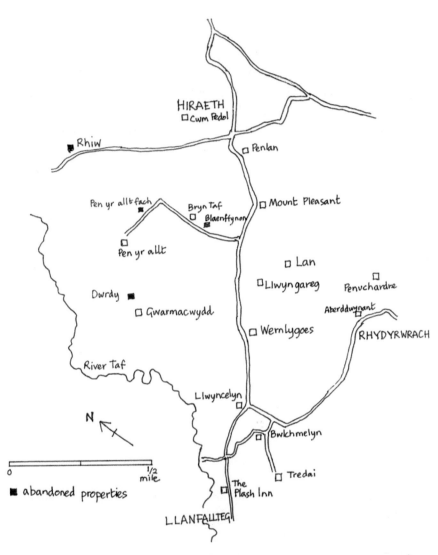

LLANFALLTEG TO HIRAETH (early 20th Century)

Parke

Parke (alternative spellings in the past include Parciau, Parcau & Parciau) was a very significant estate, with lands reaching right into the centre of Llanfallteg, even though it is in Henllan Amgoed; Llwyncelyn and Bwlchmelyn were part of the estate.

In 1744, the Poyer family owned Parke and when Catherine Poyer married Howell Davies, the Methodist cleric, they lived in Parke, which is very close to Henllan Amgoed chapel. Their only daughter, Margaret inherited the home and she married the Reverend Nathaniel Rowland, another Methodist leader and son of the well-known Daniel Rowland of Llangeitho. They continued to live at Parke until he died in 1831.

Nathaniel, their son, later inherited Parke. He was a Captain in the Carmarthenshire Yeomanry and when he died childless in 1849, he left *'Parke alias Place y Parke'* to his sister Louisa, who was the third wife of Thomas Thomas, a yeoman. As soon as Louisa inherited the house they took up residence. In 1851 when Thomas died, aged 93, their son George (1820-83) succeeded to Parke where he remained until his death. His son, Rowland Lewis Thomas, known locally as Rowley, continued living there until 1919. He was a successful medical practitioner and was the Coroner for West Carmarthenshire and Joint Master of the Pembroke and Carmarthen Otter Hounds. He died in 1949.

Rowley held a weekly surgery in the village, and Dr. Owen of Whitland held a second surgery one day a week in Hope Cottage.

When Parke was auctioned, following Rowley's death in 1949, the estate consisted of 15 properties, including Parke itself. The other properties were:

- *Pantyrhyg*
- *Llain Rhos Bica*
- *Bwlchmelyn*
- *Llwyncelyn*

- *two fields at Llwyncelyn*
- *Troedyrhiw, a freehold cottage and garden situated in Llanfallteg and occupied by Caleb Edwards at a yearly rental of £3. 5s. 0d,*
- *a cottage and garden adjoining Troedyrhiw, held on a lease for 70 years from 29th September 1865, at a rent of £1. 1s. 0d. per annum*
- *Blaen Nos at Henllan Amgoed*
- *Henllan farm of 157 acres occupied by Joseph Hancock as a yearly tenant at £225 per annum to include a commodious dwelling house, dairy, cow house for 23, calves' cottage, loose box, cart house with loft, 8 stall stable with loft over, barn, large cattle shed, implement shed, boiler house with the purchaser to pay £55 for standing timber.*
- *Caeremlyn, with Mrs Sarah Walters as a yearly tenant paying £120 per annum for a dwelling house, dairy, outer kitchen, carthouse, coach house, 5 stall stable, loose box, barn, potato house with loft over, a 19 cow house, 2 pigstyes, an implement shed and 96.881 acres.*
- *Clynfields, 29 acres of rich pasture and the yearly tenant, David Thomas paying a rent of £60 per annum for a dwelling house, dairy, cart house for 8 cows with store loft about, 2 stall stable, calves cott and pigstye and a freehold smiths shop occupied by David Rees at a rent of £5. per annum.*
- *a freehold cottage and garden known as Rhydcaeremlyn and 200 acres occupied by Edward Thomas paying a yearly rent of £3. 10s. 0d.*
- *another freehold cottage, Ty – Eglwys, occupied by David Davies at a yearly rent of £2. 10s. 0d.*
- *Hillside, three miles from Whitland, a country residence of 57.25 acres occupied by Mrs J Chidloe at a yearly rental of £30 and the fields let to Mr Hancock for £24 per annum.*

Llwyncelyn

Llwyncelyn is a ten minutes walk away from the old railway station in the centre of the village. The house sits high above the village but the land stretches down to the river Tâf, and is bisected by both the railway line and the road. Since 1974 some land to the east of, and including, the railway has been part of the farm.

The earliest date and name recorded for the property is for Thomas Phillips of Llwyncelyn being the churchwarden at St. Mallteg's Church in 1760. He was buried in the churchyard on May 17th 1783. William Parker Howell owned the 84 acres of Llwyncelyn in 1843, with John James farming the land along with servants Sarah Jenkins, 25, and Abel Evans, 15.

By 1871 Dinah Bowen was farming 80 acres here, along with dairymaid Margaret Thomas 24, and servants John Owen, 16, Esther Davies, 21, and Evan John, 26. Dinah also had two young daughters Sarah, 4, and Maria, 7. The following 20 years saw the acreage increasing to 90, with Evan John, Dinah Bowen's servant, farming here in 1891, as well as at Bwlchmelyn, where he continued living until the 1920s.

Walter Adams and his wife Elizabeth (Betsy), both 39, and their eight-month-old son, Benjamin, his sister Sarah and an agricultural labourer John Jones and a servant of 15, Robert Wilson were farming the land in 1901. John Lewis, a clergyman of 57 was also lodging with them. Walter had been a servant with Evan John in 1891 and knew the farm well. He died in October 1913, at the age of 53, leaving his wife, Betsy, to carry on farming.

Llwyncelyn

In the Parke estate sale of the 2nd July 1919, Llwyncelyn consisted of 68 plus acres of rich pasture and arable land occupied by Betsy Adams. She paid £104.14s. 0d. rent per annum. The buildings comprised of '*an excellent dwelling house, cow house for 14 cows, 5 stall stable with loft above, chaffroom, two cattle sheds, cart house, barn, straw house and pigsties*'. Betsy died in April 1939, at the age of 78.

In the 1970s, the farm boasted a fine herd of dairy cows, along with extensive indoor winter housing below the farmyard. In summertime, the cows would often be see in the centre of the village being driven up the hill for milking.

The Adams family continued to farm there until late into the 1980s when Emrys passed away. The farm was then sold to join up with Gwarmacwydd next door. Many plots were sold off in the 1980s along the roadside, spreading the village further up the hill towards the house and yard.

Bwlchmelyn

Bwlchmelyn is situated within a quarter of a mile of Llanfallteg village. It appeared on the 1831 Ordnance Survey map and tithes maps and schedule of 1843, owned by William Parker Howell. There were two dwellings at the location, although not differentiated by name. At this time it was a Smithy, with David John and wife Margaret operating the forge. They continued operating here for at least 10 years. In a second property was Sarah Evans, of independent means, with her two sons, Ben and Thomas and her daughter, Elizabeth. John James farmed the 9.2 acres that belonged to Bwlchmelyn.

1871 brought a new trade to the house in the form of the shoemaker Thomas Phillips (1836-1891) and his wife Betsy (1834 -1884). They had three children, John born 1863, William born 1865 and Mary born 1869. They continued to live and work there for another twenty years. Thomas and Betsy's son John carried on the family business of shoemaking after he married Annie and made his home at Bradford House. Thomas employed apprentices, William Williams, who worked for him as a journeyman shoemaker during the 1880s, and Thomas Salmon during the 1890s.

Bwlchmelyn

His son William also married Betsy after his fathers death. Benjamin Scourfield and Sophie lived there with them working on the land as labourers.

Evan John had worked for Dinah Bowen Jones of Gwarmacwydd as a servant and also farmed at Llwyncelyn. He took over farming at Bwlchmelyn in 1881 and later lived and farmed there until 1920. The house and farm appear as lot No 3 in the Parke estate sale of 1919. Evan John is listed as living in the house, as a yearly tenant, paying an annual rent of £20. The sale particulars describe the house and lands as: *'an excellent dwelling house, cow shed for four cows, coach house and pigsty, good meadow land and a total acreage of 7.971, the average tithe Rent being £1. 4s. 7d. And in addition the purchaser to pay an extra £18 for standing timber.'*

Born in 1842, Evan John was a deacon at Caersalem Baptist Chapel, Login for over 50 years. He often walked the 4 miles to services there. He was one of those responsible for establishing Capel Rhos, Llanfallteg in 1915. He died in 1935, aged 94.

Derek and Sarah James live at Bwlchmelyn today. The dwelling, which sits on high ground, has been renovated into a two-story house with expansive views over the countryside towards the south.

Brynglas; Tredai; Plas Rhos y Velindre; Treoslyn

Maenor Tredai was part of the de Breose estate during the early 1200s. When the Crown returned their lands, Tredai went to Eve, the wife of William de Cantelope and eventually passed to William de Clinton. Hence Tredai was to become part of the lands known as Trayne Clinton (Clinton's Third).

John Thomas lived at Tredai and became a Churchwarden at St Mallteg's Church in 1761 and again in 1773. Whilst the Thomas family were living at Tredai leases reveal that it a small estate. On the 27th September 1779, *John Protheroe of Pencraig, gent* and *William Williams, yeoman of Llwynglas, Llanddewi Velfrey* were granted a year's lease for '*Place Pen y lan, Place Rhyddoles Hesiog (now commonly called Llwynkelling} within the Manor of Treday and Blane Hiraeth in Llanfallteg Parish*'. They renewed the lease for a further year in 1790. William Williams' brother and heir, John Williams of Llanscar Hill in Narberth, together with John Howell, subsequently took out a further lease on 20th April 1786.

There is evidence that Tredai was a substantial holding. An agreement was made at the Great Sessions in Carmarthen on 1st April 1786 between Walter Rice Howell and Evan Griffith of Glanrhyd, the plaintiffs and John Howell, Esq., and Mary his wife, in respect to 4 messuages, 10 cottages, 4 barns, 4 stables, 2 smiths forges, 14 gardens, 4 orchards and 930 acres in Llanfallteg. This was a substantial part of Llanfallteg parish.

Tredai then had an association with the John family. For more than the 30 year period covered by the 1841 to 1871 census returns, John and Elizabeth John, with daughters Mary, Margaret and Martha and sons Joshua and Caleb lived at Tredai. Following this, Thomas and Martha John lived there for at least another 20 years.

By 1901, Walter and Eleanor Hughes were farming at Tredai, with sons David and Edward and daughters Emily, Phoebe, Mary and Margaret.

Between 1910 and 1926 William Gibbon farmed Tredai. While Thomas William was farming there in 1936, Tredai burnt down. A local story suggests that Thomas and his wife were lying in bed and that he complained about the noise the hailstones were making on the roof, when in fact the tiles were breaking due to the heat from the fire. When the property was rebuilt in 1938, the new owner, William Morris of Hebron renamed it 'Brynglas'. In September 1961 W.G.Toop bought the property.

Shortly afterwards, the 72.51 acres and Brynglas changed hands again with the new owner being Ronald Potter, a former SAS man from Hereford. He was tragically killed on 14th August 1969, in a tractor accident on the yard. His widow Sylvia sold Brynglas in 1970 and moved away to Scotland. She still maintains contact with the area and has been a regular visitor ever since.

Emrys Adams bought Brynglas and farmed it along with Llywncelyn, selling some 14 acres to John Edwards of Dolycoed in July 1980. By June 1981, the holding and house had reduced to 10.6 acres, its current size, and it passed to Violet Adams as part of a matrimonial settlement. Then, another Mr. and Mrs. Edwards acquired the property.

In January 1990, the Edwards sold out to John and Christine Davies from Inverness, who stayed barely a year before selling on to Clive Denton and Danielle Connolly. Dani was an enthusiastic horsewoman and Brynglas became another of the rising number of stables in the area. Clive was a gardener specialising in propagating shrubs in his poly tunnel and growing vegetables in a small field. The cowshed was converted into accommodation for holidaymakers.

Current owners, Cliff and Heather Richmond moved in May 1999 and still live at the house now. Horses no longer dominate but there is a wide range of birds of all kinds, including owls, living there.

Gwarmacwydd; Dwrdy; Madwrdy

Gwarmacwydd was originally a farm called Dwrdy in the Tâf Valley, just north of Wernlygoes. In the 18th century, Dwrdy belonged to the Protheroe family of The Grove in Narberth.

Nicholas John from Dwrdy was Churchwarden in 1785, whilst James James was Churchwarden in 1805. In 1809, William George of Lan owned the 97.1 acres and Elizabeth George occupied Dwrdy, with two servants.

The farm is shown as Madwrdy on the 1831 and 1881 Ordnance Survey maps.

Richard Bowen Jones, rector of Cilymaenllwyd from 1840, an active member of the school board and a magistrate, bought the property and built a small residence there and called it Gwarmacwydd. He lived there with his wife, Clara, young son, a cook and a nurse; he continued to live there until his death on 9th April 1887, his heir being Vaughan Bowen Jones. Living in a cottage on the land at Gwarmacwydd in 1851 was an agricultural labourer, Theodophilus Twinning and his wife Margaret, formerly of Penlan.

Richard had a coffin made long before his death, which he kept under his bed, regularly making sure that he still fitted into it. His tombstone still stands in Castell Dwyran churchyard and reads:

'Here Lie the Remains of 'A Classical Ass'
The Accursed of his Sons by the name of 'Jarass'
In the Earth he is Ammonia and Triphosphate of Calcium
On the Earth a 'Home Demon' and a 'Ferocious Old Ruffian'.

Clara was buried at Castle Dwyran Church, but there is a tablet in Llanboidy church to her memory *'she was a good woman, a dear kind and old mother – a gentlewoman in every sense and meaning of the term'.* She died aged 96.

In 1879, Castle Dwyran churchyard was tidied after the restoration of the church and a stile removed. Standing near the stile was the Voteporix stone, which was removed and taken to Gwarmacwydd, where it remained in a field, used as a cattle rubbing post. The stone was whitewashed over the years, which covered the inscribed lettering, but eventually whitewashing was discontinued and Miss Bowen Jones of Gwarmacwydd recognised the stone as being of historical value. The stone is now in the safe keeping of Carmarthen Museum, Abergwili.

David James was born at Dwrdy in about 1862 and was nicknamed *'Dai Dwrdy'*. He lived at other addresses in the area later in his life, including Adams Row, Dandderwen and possibly Waundelyn. He died at Dandderwen in 1933.

He had numerous exploits during his lifetime, which are remembered by members of the community. On one occasion he walked home via the railway line, probably having been to the Iron Duke Public House in Clynderwen, and, suddenly realising that a train was approaching and he had no time to get off the track, he just lay face down on the lines and let the train go over him, got up after it had passed and walked home. He was an expert fisherman and poached many fish from the river Tâf. On another occasion the bailiff followed him home. Knowing that he was being followed, he rushed into his home, threw the fish into the loft, slammed the door, pulled off his shoes and socks and when the bailiff knocked on the door and entered the room he found Dai soaking his feet. Dai denied catching any fish, although there was a fish that was still very much alive, bouncing over the floor in the room above. His wife clouted the fish and Dai shouted up to keep *'the boy'* quiet.

On another occasion he was paid to dig out a well. After having spent a considerable time working, he decided to visit the pub leaving his coat and spade at the freshly started well. A villager on passing thought that Dai had fallen into the diggings and he rallied a team to dig Dai out. When Dai staggered back from the pub he found his well was completed thanks to the villagers.

The School Inspector was often calling at his home to see why his children were not attending school regularly. On one particular instance Dai asked him if anything was *'going on'* between his wife and the Inspector, as the villagers were talking because he was at Dai's home so often. The Inspector never called again.

After her mother died, Sarah Caroline Jones, the daughter of Richard took over Gwarmacwydd and continued to live there until 1926 when Victoria Omega Davies took up residence.

In 1935 the Whitland Rural District Council constructed a reservoir on Gwarmacwydd lands, with water pipes of cast iron or asbestos running alongside the railway land to give Llanfallteg village its first mains water supply. Part of this pipework in 2009 is still in use supplying almost all Llanfallteg village right down to Dolycoed. Very little evidence of the rest of this water supply system can now be seen other than a small brick building in some woodland alongside the drive to the house.

Today, Gwarmacwydd is owned by David and Angela Colledge. It is an organic farm with self-catering holiday cottages, standing in 450 acres, which includes over 50 acres of ancient oak and ash woodlands with walks along the banks of the River Tâf and the trackbed of the old Cardi Bach – the Whitland to Cardigan railway.

Llwyngarreg; Blaen Foes Velen

The earliest mention we have of this farm is found on a stone in the wall of St Mallteg's Church, dedicated to '*Thomas Phillips of Kevenvarchen, the eldest son of Evan Phillips of Llwyngarreg, who departed this life in 1739 aged 52 years, also his wife, Esther, who died 20th October 1776 aged 75 years*'.   Evan Phillips was also burried in the churchyard on 9th July 1743.

Before Esther Phillips died she, her son Thomas and Lewis Phillips of Llanboidy, gent and John Thomas of Llangan, yeoman, agreed on a lease for a year of Llwyngarreg, Penyclippin and Keven Hiraeth in the Parish of Llanfallteg. By 28th November 1758, the same parties agreed to a pre-nuptial settlement of the above lands to Thomas Phillips and Elizabeth Thomas, her portion to be £150.

Mary Phillips, daughter and only child of Thomas, was baptised on 12th September 1760 at St Mallteg's church. She inherited Llwyngarreg on the death of her father on 25th July 1762. She married Rees Williams of Penrheol in Meidrim on 27th July 1785 and Tyr Velin, Gothy, Llanvinith, Llanegwad, Llwyngarreg, Tyr Penclippin and Keven Hiraeth were part of their marriage settlement. Unfortunately, Rees died within 6 months of the marriage. Mary soon remarried, her second husband being John Howell of Tegfynydd. They settled at Penrheol.

Evan Davies lived at Llwyngarreg in 1764, with his wife Elizabeth. He became churchwarden in 1769. Their daughter, Anne, married a ropemaker, John Charles, from Haverfordwest. In turn, one of their daughters, Catherine, a spinster, stayed at Llwyngarreg farming 46 acres with three servants. She died in 1849.

In the 1840s William Parker Howell owned Llwyncelyn, Penclippin, Hiraeth, Llwyngarreg, Llatch y Gorse, Gorm y hendy pellaf, Bwlchmelin, Plas y pwdel, Pengarddau, slangs in Lan and Penderi. He lived in Worcester and at Penrheol near Meidrim, and inherited a considerable amount of land locally from his step-grandmother Mary Phillips. John Howell of Tegfynydd had five children by his first wife, the eldest of whom, Morris married Louise Parker of Bromyard. William Parker Howell was their son; he served as an officer in the Worcestershire Yeomanry, rising to the rank of Lieutenant Colonel.

In 1851, John James was the farmer at Llwyngarreg, with his wife Elizabeth, two baby sons and three servants. By 1871, James Davies had taken over Llwyngarreg and lived here with his wife Mary and three young children, with three servants. By 1878, Thomas and Mary Williams with two servants were occupying 44 acres, by which time John Thomas owned it.

Enoch Adams and his sisters Rebecca and Ellen, from Llanddewi Velfrey, were farming at Llwyngarreg in 1891; followed by Luke Adams before 1920.

For the past twenty years or more the current owners, Elizabeth and Paul O'Neill have lived at Llwyngarreg, which is a substantial house set below the road. The holding is now only 12 acres and has a wonderful garden, which is frequently open to the public. A 1789 half sovereign was found in the garden in 2002.

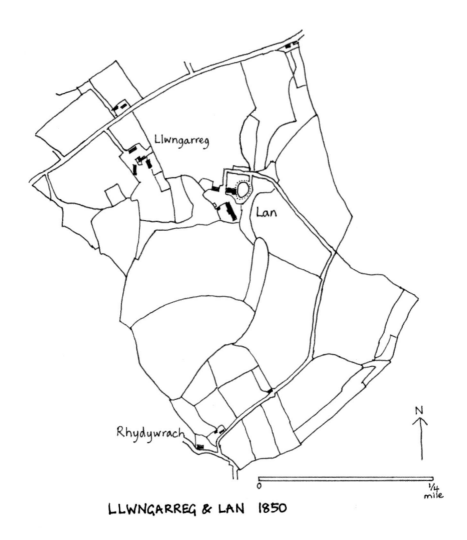

LLWNGARREG & LAN 1850

Lan; Lanrhydwilim

A document dated 7th March 1738 stated that the deceased, John Davies, gent, of Llanboidy, had owned two messuages called Lan and Trehir. Lan was a substantial estate, and originally approached by a trackway from Rhydywrach passing by Penuchardre (now derelict) in Rhydywrach.

Between 1750 and at least 1777 St Mallteg's Churchwarden, David John, lived at Lan.

William George and his wife Margaret owned and lived at Lan in 1841. By 1851, Elizabeth Evans was farming some 70 acres of the land with her son Thomas. Thomas became the Rector of St Mallteg's Church and lived at Lan along with his housekeeper Margaret Jones, and servants. By 1901, Margaret had died, but Thomas, at 88, still a clergyman, had two of his nieces, Elizabeth and Jane, looking after him along with three servants.

William George, still the owner, sold off the produce in the fields in 1859 along with the animals and chattels, for the sum of £280. Then in 1864, he sold the 245, acres along with five other properties of the Lan estate which were described as follows in the auction details of the 8th June:

'Penlan rented by Mr Theodophilus Twining as was also the Parkylan pasture. Altypercill and Rhiw were tenanted by Daniel Thomas. The rest of the estate contained ten cottages and gardens and Lan was described as a modern built and in good repair and the interior well arranged. Being well protected by rising grounds and plantations, its situation is at once mild and salubrious commanding from its elevated position extensive views far into the counties of Pembroke and Carmarthen and the house is most beautifully situated in the midst of its own ornamental trees and park like meadows. The county around is very pleasing and the neighbourhood highly respectable, situated at a short distance from two stations of the South Wales Railway the facilities of conveyance are great, and the excellent market towns of Haverfordwest, Carmarthen and Narberth conveniently accessible. The situation is exceedingly healthy and excellent shooting, fishing and field sports around combine to render it a most desirable residence. Mr Powell of Maesgwynne's celebrated pack of fox hounds hunt the immediate neighbourhood. The postage communication is good, the postman calling daily except Sundays.'

On 25th July 1913, the Lan estate was for sale once more. The house had

'dining and drawing rooms, a study, servants' hall, kitchen, outer kitchen, five bedrooms, a bathroom with hot and cold water and WC, servants bedrooms, dairies, stables, coach house, cowhouse and other outbuildings, a splendid kitchen garden, orchard, lawn, shrubbery and flower garden together with 31 acres of pastureland. The house is

supplied throughout with magnificent drinking water and is in excellent repair and the interior well arranged'.

Lot No. 2 was '*Penuchardre, the house and outbuildings commodious and convenient and in excellent repair, 54 acres and including a large new hay house'.*

Lot 3 was '*Mount Pleasant, the house substantially built with outbuildings and 29 acres'.*

Lot 4 '*Aberddwynant (commonly known as Rhydywrach) a convenient dwelling house and outbuildings, two gardens and let on a 13 year lease to run with 11 acres of meadow'.*

Lot 5 was adjoining Rhydywrach, a tumbled down cottage and garden of 0.2 acres.

Between 1914 and 1920 Jane Evans lived at Lan. She was followed by John R. Thomas, who lived there for the next three years.

Oliver Jones and his family then moved to Lan from Pantyblaidd. Oliver bred Welsh Corgis and he was the owner of Shan Fach, the first champion corgi. Another of his dogs was Champion Crymych President, which sired the first Royal corgi '*Dookie'*, given to the young Princess Elizabeth before she became Queen. Oliver went on to breed many champions which he exhibited mainly at Crufts and gained many rosettes and awards. He died in 1988 and his son Berry continues to live at Lan.

Lan (John Spencer)

Bryn Tâf

Bryn Tâf is not shown on the 1831 Ordnance Survey map, nor the parish tithe map. It was first mentioned on the 1881 census returns and its early history is closely linked to that of nearby Penrallt. Margaret, the elder daughter of Thomas and Sarah Beynon of Penrallt, had married Henry Phillips and they, along with the widowed Sarah Beynon, were farming 60 acres at Bryn Tâf.

Records show they had two servants and a carter living with them in 1901. Henry Phillips continued to farm Bryn Tâf until 1920 when John Evans took over. The Evans family went on to farm Bryn Tâf until the death of Vincent Evans in 1996, when the Morris family, the current owners, bought the property.

Penrallt

There is a gravestone at the top of the garden at Penrallt for Thomas Beynon and Jane Protheroe, who lived at Penrallt through the 1700s. Llanfallteg church records show that Thomas Beynon was the Churchwarden in 1764 and 1776. James Beynon was Churchwarden in 1795, followed by another Thomas Beynon in 1807. Thomas Beynon (died on 28th May 1832) can be traced in census records from 1841 onwards.

Gravestone of Thomas and Jane

189

In the 1840s Thomas Beynon of Penrallt was farming 44 acres, 3 roods and 24 poles and in addition to his wife, Sarah, and his first child, had two farm servants living in the house, plus two other servants sleeping over the stable. By 1851 he was farming 95 acres, had 2 daughters and a farm labourer, barnhouse maid and a housemaid.

After Thomas died, his widow Sarah continued to farm and during 1871 she was farming 100 acres with her two daughters, a general servant, a farm servant and dairymaid.

Sarah, the youngest daughter of Thomas and Sarah Beynon had married John Evans and in 1881, they were farming 87 acres at Penrallt. By this time, Sarah Beynon had moved to a new farm, Bryn Tâf, to live with her elder daughter Margaret and her husband Henry Phillips.

Penrallt

John Evans died, aged 37, in 1885 leaving Sarah a widow with 6 children. She later remarried to John Thomas. They had two servants until the children were of working age; no servants were listed in the 1901 census. John Thomas farmed Penrallt until 1923 when his stepson John Evans, who was already farming nearby Bryn Tâf took over. Alun Gibbon Evans farmed Penrallt from about 1948 to 1987, when Michael and Carol Glover bought it. Brian and Barbara Hoddesdon purchased Penrallt in 1998 and the present owners moved in in 2002.

One of the fields is affectionately named the '*Loofah - tree - field*', due to the presence of a gnarled and knobbly old oak tree. Trunk measurements suggest that the tree is over 200 years old. The 1843 Tithe Map shows this field by the River Tâf as Field Number 358, named on the schedule as *Llwyn Newydd* (New Tree Field). Welsh tradition was to bury your horse in a field and plant an oak tree to mark the spot. Certainly digging a large horse-size hole would be far easier in this field, as it is water meadow and soft marshy ground - unlike most of the other Penrallt fields, which are rab topped with a thin layer of soil.

The 'Loofah' tree

Pen-yr-allt Fach

Pen-yr-allt Fach used to be beside the track near Penrallt. This property is not shown on the 1831 Ordnance Survey map and does not appear in the census returns until 1871, when David James and his wife Hannah, both paupers, lived there. By 1881 Theophilus Twinning, a retired farmer, (formerly of Penlan) was in residence with his wife, Margaret. From 1891, through to the last records we have in 1914, the agricultural labourer Evan Davies lived there with his wife, Mary. Today there is little evidence of this building's existence - except a few daffodils and garden plants in the hedgerow of the lane where it once stood.

Blaenffynnon

Another cottage named Blaenffynnon once stood alongside the lane that runs from Bryn Tâf to the main road. This cottage has now disappeared. In the 1876 will of Sarah Beynon of Penrallt, the field schedule and properties shows that there were, in fact, two cottages and gardens here, owned by Penrallt. It can only be traced back through census records, but is not shown on the 1831 Ordnance Survey map, which was surveyed 10-15 years before publication.

In 1841, Jonathan Rees, possibly a shoemaker, lived in one cottage with his wife Elizabeth and three children. A carpenter, Benjamin Phillips, his wife Martha and their 2 children occupied the other dwelling. By 1851 there is no mention of the Phillips family, but the Rees family had grown to include 6 children. Their mother, Elizabeth, is listed as the head of household. Living with them was the 60 - year old Sarah Beynon, now a widow.

By 1871, Frances Harries, a 68-year old pauper, lived at Blaenffynnon with her son Benjamin, a labourer, and grandson Thomas, aged 11.

On the 1881 Census John Phillips, a cooper, was head of the household at Blaenffynnon with his wife Elizabeth. Frances Harries is listed as a widow and agricultural labourer in '*Blaenffynnon No.2*', along with her 36-year-old son, Benjamin.

By 1901, only Elizabeth Phillips is mentioned as living at Blaenffynnon, now aged 64 and a widow, with a living-in servant.

Nowadays there is little sign of Blaenffynnon - the present owners of Bryn Tâf (sited one field along the track from where Blaenffynnon once stood), found many steel bands from old barrels when they moved in the 1990s and never knew why. Perhaps John Phillips, the cooper from Blaenffynnon, had left behind the fruits of his labour!

Sources

Deeds and indentures of Tâf House.

Conveyance to Whitland and Tâf Vale Railway Company.

Deed of easement GWR and Whitland Rural District Council.

Llanfallteg School admission records

London Gazette

HIRAETH

The hamlet of Hiraeth sits at the northern extremity of the parish, where a wide gully with a stream runs westward into the River Tâf. The valley is particularly steep on the southern side where the road comes up from Cwm Miles, a convenient crossing point of the River Tâf at Penbontbren. Drovers would certainly have used this road; the names Penclippin and Cwmpedol have associations with shoeing livestock. Due to its topography, part of the Hiraeth area may have still been wooded after much of the rest of the parish was under cultivation. This is the highest part of the parish with steeper slopes and thinner soils.

Hiraeth in December 2007 showing some of the strip fields running down the hill. Houses are (left to right) Ffynnonau, Gwenfro and Awelfan. Fronhiraeth is in the foreground.
(John Spencer.)

Strip fields

The north side of the stream has a series of long, thin, strip fields running from the top of the hill down to the stream at the bottom, in sharp contrast to the larger squarer fields of the surrounding area. A series of strip fields forming smallholdings between Blaenhiraeth and Panty appear to have been referred to as 'Hiraeth'. Llain (which translates as 'narrow strip') was further down the valley. In 1758 Hester Phillips of Llwyngarreg agreed to a year's lease of Tyr Penclippin and Keven Hiraeth. Cefn in Welsh means ridge, or arable strip field.

The classic explanation for this type of strip field is that they were created during periods of agricultural enclosures, when dispossessed people resettled and cleared fresh ground to farm; however there was relatively little enclosure in west Carmarthenshire.

Derivation of the name

Hiraeth does not translate neatly into English; it means '*longing, grief, sorrow or nostalgia*' and it is easy to suppose that the original inhabitants used the name because they had moved reluctantly or under pressure and were pining for their old homes. In old Welsh *hyraeth* also means '*shocking or concussion*', but another old Welsh word probably explains the derivation of Hiraeth: *hyranedd* means '*divisibility, the state of being easily shared, or divided*'; it also translates as '*a long house*'. In Welsh *-dd* is pronounced *-th* in English, so *hyranedd* could easily mutate to *hiraeth*. Thus, the name for Hiraeth probably indicates that land that was shared between several people, which is consistent with the field systems and the landscape.

Welsh law, as established by Hywel Dda in the tenth century, included partible inheritance; a man's lands were divided equally between his sons, both legitimate and illegitimate. After the Acts of Union in 1536 and 1543, Welsh inheritance law was replaced with the English primogeniture law, where the eldest son solely inherited. *Hyranedd* was probably a useful concept in Welsh law, and the word has disappeared from common usage due to the legal changes in the 16th century.

When first farmed, Hiraeth may have been large arable fields with no hedge banks. Later banks delineated boundaries for the occupiers, and some of these boundaries have a slight 'S' shape indicating that they had been ploughed. The sizes of the original holdings in Hiraeth were mainly ten acres and their occupants subdivided these strips into smaller fields.

It is likely that the strips of land were shared between people working on a nearby manor or a grange belonging to Whitland Abbey, and that they were allowed to use marginal land on the edge of the estate. A lease in 1779 suggests that most of the northern part of the parish, including *Bryntafe*, Penlan and Blaenhiraeth, was part of the manor of Tredai, which once covered 1000 acres of Llanfallteg parish. Tredai would probably also have included Alltyperchyll and Rhiw, as they were later part of the Lan estate. The part of Hiraeth north of the stream in the valley was once '*bounty land*': land given by the Crown as a reward for military service. The likeliest explanation is that this land previously belonged to Whitland Abbey, and the Crown confiscated the land during the Dissolution of the Monasteries.

There is another area of small fields down in Rhydywrach by the River Tâf around Lletty, where there is another holding called Llain, which was almost certainly once part of Tredai. Cottagers working on the manor would have lived here and the area may have been divided up for them in much the same way as it was in Hiraeth.

There is evidence that the road from the Hiraeth crossroads to Llanboidy is newer than the other roads; it cuts through two of the strips, rather than going round them. The old entrance to Cwmpedol used to be down a steep track on the Cwm Miles road and only in the latter part of the 20th century has the entrance been altered so that there is suitable access for vehicles from the Llanboidy road.

The tithe maps of the 1820s show some fields with the characteristic curve on the headlands where an ox plough turned. Each occupant would have had a *cefn* to farm, and over time they would have split the *cefn* into small fields. This is strong evidence that people were farming in Hiraeth before the Black Death, as the landscape of strip fields is a relic of the early medieval feudal system, where serfs were allowed to have their own plot of land in return for working on the manor.

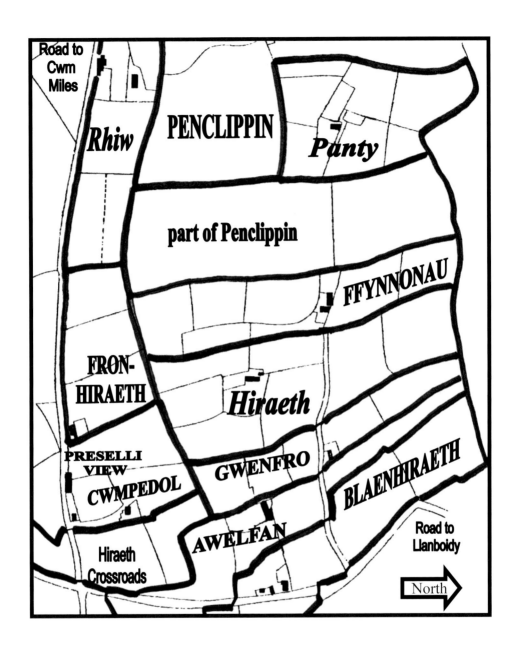

Map illustrating the tithe schedules of 1843
Note the long thin strips of land, subdivided into small fields. Also
note the slight curves along some of the long hedge lines, where ox
ploughs turned.

KEY TO MAP

Map of Hiraeth based on the 1843 tithe maps, showing the holdings and their fields. The Hiraeth crossroads is in the bottom left corner, with west being at the top of the page. The land boundaries are largely similar to today, except for Cwmpedol.
Names in capitals exist today, lower case holdings have disappeared.

Blaenhiraeth. The road to Llanboidy cuts through this *cefn* and the neighbouring one belonging to Awelfan, indicating that the road is *'relatively'* new, although it has been there for centuries.

Awelfan. Referred to as Hiraeth until the 20th century.

Gwenfro. Like Awelfan, referred to as Hiraeth until the 20th century, then as Hiraeth East after Awefan and Ffynnonau were named.

Hiraeth. Latterly Hiraeth West, now derelict and part of Ffynnonau since 1936. There is evidence of a *'fulling site'* here.

Ffynnonau. Originally referred to as Hiraeth, previous owners have acquired neighbouring land on either side.

Part of Penclippin. Penclippin Farm's land is further down the valley and above the Cwm Miles road. This strip became part of Ffynnonau in 1880. These fields have, contrary to the trend elsewhere, been divided to match field sizes on the rest of the farm.

Panty (or Pantau). Now derelict, the land was purchased by Ffynnonau in 1929. There is evidence of a *'fulling site'* here.

Rhiw. Now derelict, this land is now included in the Fronhiraeth holding. It was part of the Lan estate at the time of the tithe map.

Fronhiraeth. Previously known as Alltyperchyll. Now includes the land from Rhiw. Also previously part of the Lan estate.

Preseli View. Originally there was a house called Plevna on this site.

Cwmpedol. Originally owned by Lan, the holding in 1843 farmed different fields to today. One field has been transferred to Fronhiraeth and the fields near the crossroads have been included. Originally, the track to Cwmpedol ran down the steep hill past Preseli View from the Cwm Miles road; nowadays it is approached on a lesser gradient from the Llanboidy road.

There is a dearth of documented evidence on the people who lived in Hiraeth: there were no estates or significant farms to generate wealth, and consequently little need to record wills or contracts. The smallholdings were no more than subsistence farms and the early incumbents would have worked on the Abbey land or a manor, working on their own land for one day a week.

After the end of the Napoleonic Wars grain prices fell, making the local estates less profitable. Consequently the need for casual agricultural labourers was reduced. People who did not move to work in the growing mines or steel industry had to utilise other skills to support a family, such as making clothing and footwear.

Nearly all the holdings were rented or leased, often annually, so tenure could be a problem. *Clogyfran* and *Blaen-hyraeth* were sold at auction in 1866: Mrs Walters of *Clogyfran*, Thomas Lewis who rented four acres at *Blaen-hyraeth* for £8 8s 0d, and Thomas Rees who occupied the cottage and garden there, were given notice to quit prior to the sale.

Benjamin and Mary Thomas had been farming Penclippin for some years before they bought *Tyr Penclippin, Keven Hiraeth and Hiraeth* from William Parker Howell in 1857 for £1950. Also included in the sale was Pengarddu, occupied by Sarah Evans. Benjamin died a year later, but his widow continued to farm at Penclippin.

Ffynnonau

In 1857 Ffynonnau was described as a *messuage tenement farm pieces or parcel of land buildings hereditaments + premises commonly called & known by the name of Hiraeth 8a 2r 12p* which was occupied by Anne Evans.

Mary Thomas of Penclippin received £250 compensation in 1870 when the railway crossed her land. This money and the railway moving slate from Glogue quarry may have allowed her to build Ffynnonau farmhouse, with the old stone and *clom* cottage being relegated to buildings for the farm. Previous records listed the property as *Hiraeth*, along with several other houses.

Mary moved into Ffynnonau when she retired from farming, her son Evan taking over at Penclippin. In 1879 Mary Thomas died, and her daughter Margaret and new husband Daniel Davies inherited Ffynnonau and the neighbouring strip *Kevenhiraeth*. They had a clergyman as lodger, so they had some disposable income, which enabled them to pay the mortgage that was still outstanding from the original purchase of the land from William Parker Howell.

Some improvements were made to the land around this time. Small land drains were put in (possibly with pipes from Llanfallteg brickworks) and some hedges were removed. Daniel Davies also worked as a haulier and there is evidence that part of the farm buildings were modified and converted to a cart-shed. He probably moved goods to and from the railway station in Llanfallteg.

Daniel and Margaret moved to Whitland and rented out the land on an annual tenancy for a couple of years. In December 1892 W. John Sampson, a local labourer's son from Cwm, in his mid 20s, who had trained to be a teacher, bought the property for £903-3-0. He taught in Henllan Amgoed school as well as farming.

John Sampson moved to Panteg in 1921 when John Richards purchased Ffynnonau, at a time when prices for farm produce and farmland were low. Over the next decade he purchased the strips on each side, effectively doubling the size of the farm. The houses on both the newly purchased holdings (Hiraeth and Panty) were abandoned and the occupants of both moved locally. John Richards had built Ffynnonau into a viable small family farm, which was taken over in 1957 by his son Eric and wife Margaret.

Further land '*improvements*' were made during the 1960s. The Small Farm Scheme paid farmers to remove hedges, which were bulldozed out, although the position of the old hedges is still given away by small ridges and lines of daffodils. Nowadays farmers are subsidised to plant hedges.

Ffynnonau had milking cows until 1979 when, like many other dairy farms, milking stopped with the withdrawal of milk churn collections. The churn stand is still at the farm entrance where it is now used for the refuse bags. Increased agricultural mechanisation and cheaper produce demand larger land areas for farms to be viable, so Ffynnonau is now uneconomical as a stand-alone farm.

Shoemaking

Several people in Hiraeth made a living from shoemaking during Victorian times. John Williams of Llain and his two sons were cobblers. The eldest son, Morris, worked at home, whilst the younger son, William, worked for Thomas Phillips of Bwlchmelyn. Their neighbour, Ben Davis of *Rhyd-fach,* was also a shoemaker. His son Benjamin learnt his trade with David Owens of *Pennsylvania-isaf,* who was a clog maker. Clogs were widely used in rural areas until cheap boots from the English Midlands arrived by rail. The local shoemakers probably obtained some of their raw materials from the tannery in Cwm Miles.

The Woollen Industry

Textile manufacture was another important source of revenue for many cottagers to have during the nineteenth century. There were weavers living and working at *Ty-newydd* (now Prescelli View) and *Blaenhiraeth*. Edward (born 1776) and Ann Phillip lived at *Ty-newydd*, whilst Benjamin Phillips operated from Blaenhiraeth. He and his wife Sophia had two surviving children, although they buried seven children between the ages of 18 months and nine. John John of *Plas-y-golin* and William David of *Pen-y-graig* were tailors at the same period.

Most women would have spent any spare time knitting or sewing, although some had no choice but to try to make their living from these skills. Rachel Llewellyn of *Troed-y-rhiw* had to support her young family by knitting stockings, following the death of her husband William in March 1881 aged 25.

Carding, spinning and cloth weaving were amongst the early domestic arts. The beginnings of the industry go back to the times of Hywel Dda when skilled Flemish weavers arrived. Even then, finished cloth was sold at local fairs and exported as far as Spain and Portugal, France and Italy.

**Spinning wheel on show in the Welsh House
at Scolton Museum**

Pandy is Welsh for *'fulling mill'*; *Pantau* on the track to
Gwarmacwydd, and *Panty* in Hiraeth are associated with fulling and
there is evidence to support this at Panty and at another site in Hiraeth.
These local fulling sites were all at the heads of small streams with a
constant but very limited flow of running water. They were very
small-scale operations and would only have supported a handful of
textile workers.

Clay (*'Fuller's earth'*) and urine (called *'wash'*) would have been
used to help clean the wool, which probably had to be left for several
days to soak in a pool. Regular pounding by walking on the wool, or
using hands or clubs, was required to clean the wool before carding
and spinning. Wales is blessed with plentiful supplies of swift
running water and so many fulling mills, powered by water wheels
were set up between 1540 and 1700. The nearest *'proper'* fulling
mill was at *Felin Cwrt* between Cwm Miles and Llandissilio.

Ruined cottage at Hiraeth with possible fulling site. Note the silted up pool draining beside the building

Welsh Dress

Naturally wool was used for clothing. Women did not show much hair but confined it with a short cap rounded over the ears and tied under the chin. A simple cape or wrap was thrown over shoulders, usually a square piece of flannel, a jacket or a blouse, a petticoat and a tall black beaver hat used on occasions.

In his diary on the 2nd August 1778, Sir T. Gery Cullen wrote, '*The inhabitants of these wretched huts are better clothed than the tenants of the better houses in England. Their woollen clothes are not so subject to end in tatters as the slight stuffs and linen of the English*'.

Welsh Costumes.

Welsh dress

Decline of cottage industries

During the first half of the twentieth century, the woollen industry declined steeply across Wales. Goods could be transported in cheaply by rail. Cotton clothes and changes in fashion led to lower demand for flannel and woollen clothing. Likewise, cheaper footwear wrecked the market for the local cobblers and clog makers. These cottage industries could not compete with mass produced clothing and these workers were the last '*hurrah*' of their craft: several houses were abandoned in Hiraeth in the early part of the 20th century.

An academic report in 1925 stated that the decline of the textile industry was due to a number of instances:

1. competition with other industries for labour,

2. changes in fashion, especially underclothes which resulted in a reduction of woven woollen fabrics,

3. the introduction of cheaper and more attractive fabrics and the sale of ready made articles.

Modern Hiraeth

The advent of easy travel by car and household utilities has led to more houses being built from the 1970s above the crossroads, helping to repopulate the area. Hiraeth now has a number of '*hobby farmers*' or '*lifestylers*' who keep a few livestock or horses, enjoying the benefits of a rural life without the deprivation and hard work that the previous occupants in earlier times had to endure.

Sources

Crankshaw *Survey of the Welsh Textile Industry*, University of Wales, 1925

Jones, Francis, *Historic Houses of Carmarthenshire and their Families*, Newport, 1997.

Pughe, William Owen. *A Dictionary of the Welsh Language, Explained in English,* Thomas Gee, London 1832

GLOSSARY

Length

A rod used for measurement was based on the length of an ox goad. A furlong was a *'furrow long'* and was the distance that an ox team ploughed between turns.

Rod, Pole & Perch = 5.5 yards = approx 5 metres
Chain = 22 yards = 4 rods = $1/10^{th}$ furlong = 20 metres
Furlong = 220 yards = 200 metres
Mile = 8 furlongs

Land Area

An acre was an area that was considered a day's work to plough for one man and an ox team. An acre is just under the size of a football pitch.

Perch = a square rod (5.5 yards by 5.5 yards)
Rood = 40 perches (1 furlong by one rod)
Acre = 4 roods (1 furlong by four rods)

Money

Penny (d). There are 12 in a shilling, 240 in a pound (£)
Shilling (s). There are 20 in a pound (£) = Equivalent to 5p today
Guinea = 21 shillings
Sovereign = Gold coin that used to be worth £1

Weight

Pound (lb). 2.2lbs in a kilogram
Hundredweight (cwt). 50 kilograms